C000131849

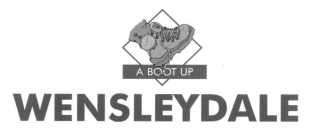

A BOOT UP

WENSLEYDALE

Keith Wood

First published in Great Britain in 2010

British Library Cataloguing-in-Publication Data
A CIP record for this title is available from the British Library

ISBN 978 1 906887 97 1

PiXZ Books
Halsgrove House, Ryelands Industrial Estate,
Bagley Road, Wellington, Somerset TA21 9PZ
Tel: 01823 653777
Fax: 01823 216796
email: sales@halsgrove.com

An imprint of Halstar Ltd, part of the Halsgrove group of companies
Information on all Halsgrove titles is available at: www.halsgrove.com

Printed and bound China by Toppan Leefung Printing Ltd

Contents

How to use this book

Wensleydale, the central of the three main dales running through the Yorkshire Dales National Park, offers both easy and more challenging walking in magnificent surroundings. The wide green U-shaped glacial valley is overlooked by the high flat topped fells of Addlebrough and Wether Fell. Unlike the majority of the Yorkshire Dales, which are named after their main rivers, the valley is named after the market town of Wensley. Until the beginning of the 18th century the valley was known as Yoredale, or Uredale after its river, the Ure.

This collection of walks is concentrated along Upper and Middle Wensleydale between Hawes and West Witton. Hawes is the main settlement and tourist centre with the Yorkshire Dales National Park Centre and is home to the Wensleydale Creamery -the makers of the only real Wensleydale Cheese. Further along the dale the still waters of Semer Water lie hidden to the south of the main valley and still further down the valley the imposing medieval fortress of Castle Bolton dominates the scene.

The valley is characterised by the green fields and hay meadows which are a profusion of colour in the early summer, enclosed by drystone walls containing a vast array of field barns.

A number of tributary valleys including Sleddale, Raydale and Bishopdale together with a variety of becks and streams drain into the main River Ure. All this water combined with the hilly terrain and the nature of the geology in the area has created a feast of waterfalls including Aysgill, Hardraw and Mill Gill Forces, Aysgarth and Redmire Falls all of which are visited on the walks in this book.

Each route is graded from Easy to More Challenging with further details of distance, height ascended and the type of terrain covered, to help with decisions of which walk to choose. The information blocks have distances and height gained in both imperial and metric measures, whereas in the body of the text I have kept to the old imperial units which still feel more appropriate (and comfortable) when describing the walks.

All ten walks are covered by the Ordnance Survey Explorer Map OL: 30 Yorkshire Dales, Northern and Central areas, and Harvey's Dales North maps. The maps in this book are only an outline version of each walk and the detail provided by the OS maps puts each route in context. Every year tens of thousands of visitors enjoy the dales with the vast majority coming to no harm. However there are many cases each year where walkers are injured, get lost or find themselves in some other kind difficulty requiring the assistance of the Rescue Services. A few simple precautions should help avoid any problems:

If you are unsure about your fitness start with the walks graded Easy and work your way up to More Challenging.

Wear suitable footwear- properly fitted walking boots are recommended for all the walks. Take suitable clothing; the weather in the Yorkshire Dales can change very quickly, take a waterproof and extra warm layers to wear. Take plenty to eat and drink en route, dehydration and lack of nourishment can lead to fatigue and mistakes being made.

An outline map illustrates each walk but it is recommended that a complete map is taken.

Inform someone of your planned route and expected return time.

Check the weather forecast in advance and only take to the more challenging routes on clear days.

And finally keep to the paths and watch where you are putting your feet – most accidents are caused by careless slips!

Useful websites:

Yorkshire Dales National Park
www.yorkshiredales.org.uk
Yorkshire Dales Society
www.yds.org.uk
Yorkshire Dales Millennium Trust
www.ydmt.org
Out of Oblivion Yorkshire Dales Heritage and Archaeology
www.outofoblivion.org.uk
Yorkshire Dales Tourism
www.yorkshiredalesand harrogate.com
Traveldales – Public Transport Information
www.traveldales.org.uk
Keith Wood Photography
www.keithwoodphotography.co.uk

Key to Symbols Used

Level of difficulty:

Easy 🍀

Fair 🍀 🍀

More challenging 🍀 🍀 🍀

Map symbols:

🚗 Park & start

⎯⎯ Tarred Road

- - - - - Footpath

■ Building / Town

🪣 Pub

▲ Landmark

Walk Locations

1 2 Gayle
3 Burtersett
4 Bainbridge
5
6 Askrigg
7 Thornton Rust
8
9 Castle Bolton
10 West Witton
Aysgarth

1 Aysgill Force from Gayle

Visit a cracking little waterfall along Gayle Beck

Gayle Beck rises in the valley of Sleddale taking water from the slopes of Dodd Fell and Wether Fell the two hills on either side of the valley. The beck flows through the village of Gayle from which it takes its name before flowing through Hawes to finally join the River Ure just past Haylands Bridge *(see Walk 2)*. Roughly half way along its length the beck descends a vertical drop called Aysgill Force and this is the highlight of this delightful walk from Gayle. The walk starts close to The Wensleydale Creamery famous for its range of crumbly Wensleydale Cheese and the makers of the only real Yorkshire Wensleydale Cheese — well worth a visit at the end of the walk.

Level:
Length: 3¼ miles (5.2km)
Ascent: 350 feet (105m)
Terrain: Field paths and an unsurfaced lane for the return
Park and Start: Public Car Park on Gayle Lane GR969 897
Info: Toilets at start, various refreshments in Hawes
www.gaylemill.org.uk,
www.wensleydale.co.uk

Ten End Hill across the hay meadows

7

Four way sign near the start of the walk

points the way through an iron kissing gate onto the green path rising through the meadows. Head towards a wall stile through the middle of the wall at the end of the first field.

(1) Park in the Richmondshire District Council Car Park on Gayle Lane, just around the back of the Hawes Primary School. Leave the car park onto Gayle Lane and turn left to walk along the pavement up the road towards Gayle past the Wensleydale Creamery. Continue along the road into the village of Gayle.

(2) Just before the bridge over Gayle Beck take the road to the right at the red wall mounted Post Office collection box and then immediately left up the road through the back of the village. Pass the ford over the beck down on the left, but keep straight on through the village. Just past the last house on the left a fingerpost indicating "Footpath"

(3) There is a four way fingerpost at the wall stile; take the path signed "FP Aysgill Force ½ mile" which is the left hand path through the next field. Go through the wall stile at the end of the next field and following the waymarker the route veers off to the left down a stepped path heading down to the banks of Gayle Beck. The narrow path gradually descends along the edge of some trees before dropping down to the banks of the beck. Follow the green path

Wall stile through the meadows

Pennine Way

Pennine Way

through the hay meadows following Gayle Beck upstream. The path passes through a bank which has had a land-slip but the route has been safely remade across the bank. It's now easy walking through the meadows beside the tree-lined Gayle Beck.

(4) The path proceeds along the top of the steep-sided gorge as Aysgill Force is approached and

the sound of the water increases in volume as the falls are reached. The waters of Gayle Beck come down as a single curtain down a rock face in a wooded glade. Now continue on the path following the banks of the beck upstream. Pass by a metal footbridge over the beck and a multi directional sign, but just keep straight on follow-ing the clear path beside the beck. Keep quiet and you are just as likely

to see grouse and hares as well as rabbits along the route. Once over a couple of high ladder stiles pass by the lonely West Close Barn and a metal footbridge. Just keep heading upstream along the right hand bank of the beck through these upland meadows with Swinesett Hill up on the right. Nearing the far end of the route pass through a gate with stone pillar gateposts and cross one last field.

(5) At the far end of the field join the farm track and turn right to head up to the gate through the wall to join a clear track. Turn right through the gate to walk along the clear track back towards Gayle with a copse of trees just ahead on the hill-side to the front left. The track passes

Ten End through the stone gateway

through numerous gated fields. As the track transforms into an enclosed lane the copse of trees and a lime kiln are passed on the left. The now unsurfaced lane starts to drop down to Hawses and some modern farm buildings are passed.

The water-powered Gayle Mill was built in 1785 to spin cotton. It evolved into a sawmill and pioneering generator of electricity from the 1879 Williamson Turbine. Close to dereliction in 2004, the mill was restored and opened to the public in 2008 in large part due to the publicity gained from the BBC 'Restoration' series.

Aysgill Force

6 Arriving at Faw Head cottage and Faw Head Barn continue on the lane, pass by a stone barn onto a surfaced road and immediately take the path through the fields signed "Pennine Way FP West End". Walk through a couple of meadows and then join the route of the outward journey to simply retrace the outward route through Gayle and back to the start. Alternatively if you have the time you could make the detour just over the bridge in Gayle to visit the restored Gayle Mill.

Re-enter the hay meadows

2 Hardraw Force from Hawes

Walk through the fields to visit England's largest single drop waterfall

Hardraw Force is reputed to be England's highest unbroken waterfall, falling some 100 feet (or 30m). The waters pour over a miniature Malham Cove type canyon known as Hardraw Scaur. The great impressionist artist JMW Turner visited in 1816 and his finished water colour of the falls is housed in the Fitzwilliam Museum, Cambridge. The falls which are accessed through the Green Dragon Inn, where a small charge is made, are an essential feature of this walk.

Starting from the National Park Car Park in Hawes where the Dales Countryside Museum is also to be found, the route makes its way through the fields to Hardraw, before heading down the dale to the hamlet of Sedbusk.

Level:
Length: 4 miles (6.4km)
Ascent: 300 feet (90m)
Terrain: Typical dales field paths
Park and Start: Yorkshire Dales National Park Car Park, Hawes GR 875 898
Info: Toilets at start, refreshments from The Green Dragon Inn, Hardraw
www.hardrawforce.com

Field boundary

13

Haylands Bridge

1 Park in the Yorkshire Dales National Park Car Park at the Dales Museum adjacent to the Ropemakers in Hawes. Leave the Car Park and walk back onto the main road past the Ropemakers. Turn right onto the main road and then immediately right again to walk along the road signed to Hardraw and Muker.

2 At the first road on the left into the Upper Wensleydale Business Park take the flagged path through the kissing gate and the meadows straight ahead signposted "Pennine Way FP Haylands Bridge ¼ mile". Keep to the flagged path which runs along the edge of the field. The path rejoins the road at Haylands Bridge over the River Ure. Cross over

Meadow scene

the bridge and then continue along the road with the river on the left. Pass by the confluence of the River Ure and Gayle Beck. The limestone scar of High Clint is straight ahead on the horizon.

The earliest records of ropemaking in Hawes date back to 1725. The current business was founded in the 1830s by the Wharton family and was sold to WRA Outhwaite in 1905. Outhwaite moved the business to the current site in 1911 where the business still thrives today making rope, cord and braid.

3 Take the next gate on the left for the path through the fields signposted "FP Hardraw ¾ mile". The path goes across the field to a bend in the river where a fingerpost reassuringly points the way forward to Hardraw. The green path proceeds along the edge of a number of fields passing through gates and stiles heading towards Hardraw with Hawes in view to the left. A waymarker points over a stone stile and the path cuts across the corner of the next field and then through a gate to join a flagged path which follows the route of the Pennine Way into Hardraw. After passing through another couple of fields the path emerges in the middle of Hardraw opposite the Green Dragon Inn.

(4) To visit Hardraw Force pass through the Green Dragon Inn. There is a small charge to pay to visit the falls at the inn. A clear path leads out the back of the inn to visit the falls. The single spout of water pouring over the scaur dropping 100 feet is an impressive sight. To continue the walk head back out through the inn and turn left immediately up the lane beside the inn signed "FP Simonstone ⅓ mile" and then follow the sign to Simonstone through the back of a yard and then through a gate onto a flagged path leading up through the fields to "Simonstone ¼ mile". The path rises along the field side, up a set of steps, over a stile and then continues up

Hardraw Force

Hardraw

more steps through the next meadow. Pass through the yard of West House following the waymarkers pointing to "Simonstone and Sedbusk". Continue across the meadows heading towards the Simonstone Hotel.

5 The path emerges just in front of the Simonstone Hotel onto the hotel drive, turn right and walk along the drive past some cottages and arriving at the "main" road go 10 yards to the left and then follow the

fingerpost "FP Sedbusk ½ mile" pointing the way through a series of gates through the meadows. Initially walking along a farm track pass by a large collection of stone farm buildings. The distinctive shape of Addlebrough hill can be seen ahead in the distance. The path now proceeds in a straight line through a patchwork of traditional drystone-wall enclosed pastures with stone barns passing through a variety of gates and stiles along the way. The succession of wall stiles increasingly narrow as Sedbusk is approached.

6 On reaching the penultimate field just before Sedbusk the path forks, take the path down to the right to the bottom corner of the field where a gated stile emerges onto a narrow lane. Just 10 yards to the right a signpost points through another gated stile back to Haylands Bridge half a mile away. With Hawes and the bridge in view the path descends quite steeply through the first field and then

over another couple of stiles through the fields. Taking care as you go straight across a road and then follow the sign again "Public Footpath Haylands Bridge" still signed as being ½ mile away on a clear path through a large field heading towards the

river. The path crosses over an ancient packhorse bridge in the last field before emerging back on the busy road. All that remains is to follow the road back over Haylands Bridge and then retrace your steps of the outbound route back to Hawes.

Path back to Haylands Bridge

3 Wether Fell

Great views from around Wether Fell

Wether Fell is the highest hill which directly overlooks Wensleydale. At 2014 feet (614m) it just tops the 2000 foot barrier. Together with the adjacent Yorburgh, the two fells dominate the Upper Wensleydale scene looking down onto the town of Hawes. This route which comes within 60 feet of the top traces an ellipse around the upper slopes of Wether Fell, avoiding the worst of the peat hags which cover the summit plateau.

Around the back of the fell the route joins the Roman Cam High Road which overlooks Raydale and Semer Water. Save this one for a clear day to enjoy the extensive views from this high level route.

Level: 🥾 🥾 🥾
Length: 5½ miles (9km)
Ascent: 1100 feet (330m)
Terrain: Steady climb up Wether Fell
Park and Start: Limited off road parking on Burtersett High Lane GR890 892
Info: No facilities on route

Looking down onto Semer Water

Hawes

A684

Burtersett 1

Gayle

2

Yorburgh

▲ Roman Road

5

3

Wether
Fell

4

1 Park at any number of suitable off road locations at the top end of the village of Burtersett. Take the "No Through Road" past the Burtersett Institute heading out of the top of the village. Follow the Public Bridleway up the unsurfaced lane to the left signed "Wether Fell 2 miles" past Greystones Cottage. Once out of the back of the village go through the gate and continue on the clear lane as it already begins its ascent up the hillside. As height is gradually gained extensive views across Wensleydale open out. Passing through a gate the track narrows and becomes rougher underfoot as it continues to steadily rise up the flanks of Wether Fell.

Burtersett

Yorburgh and Wensleydale

2 The path swings around to the left and the flat topped dome of Wether Fell comes into sight straight ahead. Ignore the farmers' track off to the right through a gate but continue on the now green path straight on aiming for the outside corner of a walled enclosure where the short cropped green path continues on the level across the open moorland. Pass a ruined hut and through a gate in the wall where the path starts to rise again swinging around to the right up the upper slopes. As height is gained there is a fine view to the left down the dale past Yorburgh and Yorburgh Hole and along Wensleydale. The green path levels off as it continues on its way to Wether Hill.

3 Go through a final gate in the wall around the top of the hill where the path turns to the right and follows the line of the wall around the top of Wether Fell. The path passes an ancient quarry with the remains of one or two lime kilns. The view up Wensleydale opens out again. Just keep to the narrow path just above the wall all the way around the fell top. Rounding the nose of the fell the path becomes wet in places especially after rain and weaves its way around an array of dark brown peat hags. The road from Wensleydale to Wharfedale comes into view overlooked by Dodd Fell.

4 Coming to the end of the wall the path joins the wide stony track of the Roman Cam High Road and the view opens out down onto Semer Water with the distinctive nose of Addlebrough just beyond. It's straight easy walking following in the footsteps of the Romans for the next mile and a half on this high level track with extensive views. Approaching a set of walls with a pair of gates keep on the main track heading down the hill. Keeping to the walled lane the track starts to descend down the hill straight as a die eventually leading to the village of Bainbridge and the start of Walk 4.

Wensleydale

5 As the track levels off with Green Scar on the right a cross roads of paths is reached; take the left hand path leaving the road signed "FP Burtersett 1 mile". Follow the faint green path which leads straight down the fellside back to the start. Cross the twin streams marking

Cam High Road runs from the Roman fort at Bainbridge all the way to Ingleton and in common with most Roman roads runs in a straight line only deviating to skirt around the highest hill tops. In the late 18th century the road was resurfaced and formed part of the Richmond to Lancaster turnpike.

Cam High Road

the top of Horton Gill either side of a wall into the second enclosure. The path loses height all the way down through these half a dozen or so fields. Cross Burtersett High Pasture and the spring of High Rigg Well with good views back up to Yorburgh and continue on the clear path down the fellside through the stiles in the walls which mark the enclosures. Approaching Burtersett the path steeply descends to the right of a small pine plantation. The path slants across the field next to the plantation to end up at bottom corner of the trees; aim for a gate through the wall. Finally it's straight down through three more fields to emerge back onto the road at the back of the village.

Through the gate and back to the start

4 Cam High Road and Semer Water

Follow in the footsteps of Romans to visit Semer Water

This is the second route, following in the footsteps of Romans on the Cam High Road. The road leads from the Roman Fort at Bainbridge. The 2 acre site named VIROSIDVM or "the settlement of true men" is believed to have been founded around AD71 and was deep in territory held by the Brigantes. The road in true Roman fashion runs almost straight as a die

Level: 🥾 🥾 🥾
Length: 5¾ miles (9km)
Ascent: 950 feet (290m)
Terrain: Steady pull up lanes returning along field paths
Park and Start: Parking beside Bainbridge Village Green GR 933 901
Info: Toilets and refreshments in Bainbridge

all the way to Ingleton. The walk itself initially goes through the fields above the River Bain before following the Roman Road for nearly a mile and a half. A short pull up the modern Crag Side Road leads to views down onto Semer Water before finally returning along the banks of the River Bain.

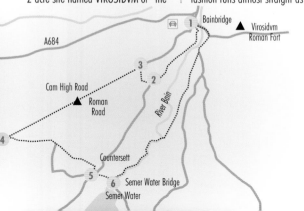

Central Wensleydale from near the start

① Park next to the village green in the middle of Bainbridge. At the southern end of the village just before the bridge follow the lane past Hazel's Roost B&B and take the lane on the right signed "FP Semer Water 2m Public Footpath" up the lane around the back of the village. Follow the waymarker sign out of the back of the village on a green path rising through the first field. The path rises with the River Bain below on the left. Keep to the green path through the hay meadows passing through two gate stiles. Passing a large field barn the route gently rises uphill through the next field. A finger post reassures us that we heading in the right direction pointing the way to Gill Edge through the next field.

② Arriving at the lane at Gill Edge through a gate, turn right signed "FP to Lane" where there are wide views up and down the length of Wensleydale. Turn right at the junction with the "main" road to walk back downhill for a ¼ of mile to meet up with Cam High Road.

Green Scar Crag from Bracken Hill

3 At a bend in the road an unsurfaced lane doubles back, this is the start of Cam High Road built by the Romans, signed "Byway Beggarmans Road 5 ½". Keep to this enclosed unsurfaced lane which heads straight as a die over the slopes of Wensleydale. This ancient highway gently rises across the hillside giving outstanding views along Wensleydale. Whilst the OS shows a path heading up to the left to cut off the corner, it is not apparent on the ground so continue along Cam High Road until you meet the surfaced Crag Side Road.

Yorburgh from Cam High Road

4 Upon reaching the road turn left to continue walking up the hillside. As the road rounds the corner at the top of the hill the nose of Addlebrough fills the view ahead. As the road swings around to the right

Cam High Road

Semer Water

a path goes straight on through a gate signed "FP Countersett ½ mile" down the hill. The path goes straight down this first field keeping the wall just on the right. Over a wall stile and Semer Water comes into view down below and the path continues heading straight down the next field. Half way down the field the path veers off to left towards a barn, through a narrow wall stile and then down the next field. Follow the way-marker to go over a stream and into the next field. And down to gate in the corner of the last field onto an unsurfaced lane around the back of the hamlet of Countersett, where in another 20 yards the road is reached.

Semer Water Bridge

Countersett Meeting House

(5) The main route continues by turning right. However it's worth making a minor detour down the road to the left to visit the early-eighteenth-century Quaker Meeting House. Turn right to head down the road signed to Stalling Busk and Marsett and then immediately left on the road down the hill towards the foot of Semer Water. The road drops steeply down to the bridge over the River Bain which is the outflow from Semer Water.

(6) Immediately over the bridge turn left through the gate to take the footpath along the banks of the Bain signed "Footpath to Bainbridge 2 miles". Follow this delightful green path along the right hand bank of the young River Bain heading back towards the village. Over a large ladder stile the path moves away from the river and starts to gently rise to climb over Bracken Hill. After a climb the rounded top of the hill is reached with Gill Edge on the opposite side of the valley. The tops of the buildings of Bainbridge can now be seen below; continue following the green path down the other side of the hill towards Bainbridge following the fingerpost signs all the way back to the village. The path emerges onto the main road just before the bridge. Simply walk back across the village green to the start.

There is a long tradition of Quakerism in Wensleydale dating to the early visits of George Fox in the 1650s. Early meetings were held in the nearby Countersett Hall and Countersett Meeting House was first built in 1710 with subsequent improvements in 1772 and remains unchanged since then.

River Bain

5 Semer Water Circuit

A high level circuit of Semer Water with great views

Semer Water is the second largest natural lake in Yorkshire. At an altitude of 815 feet (250m) it lies in a glaciated limestone valley and is a designated Site of Special Scientific Interest (SSSI). The lake is a haven for birds throughout the year including redshank, lapwing, curlew, mallard and widgeon. The meadows at the head of the lake around the hamlets of Stalling Busk and Marsett are managed as traditional hay meadows where a profusion of buttercups, clover and daisies can be seen in early summer. The walk itself is a circuit of the lake initially alongside the lake and through the meadows to Marsett where there is a stiff climb up the hillside onto the ridge which overlooks Semer Water's western shoreline.

Level: ♥ ♥ ♥
Length: 5¼ miles (9km)
Ascent: 1025 feet (310m)
Terrain: Stiff climb up to the ridge above Semer Water
Park and Start: Semer Water Foreshore Car Park GR921 975
Info: No facilities on route

Sunlight on Stalling Busk

31

Reflections in Semer Water

Field barn near the start

1 Start from the private car park at the foreshore of Semer Water below Countersett. The car park operates on a pay and display principle; tickets should be bought from Low Blean Farm ¼ mile along the lane, drive to the farm, pay for your parking and drive back to the foreshore parking to start the walk.

Leave the parking area heading right along the lane towards Low Blean Farm over Little Ings Bridge.

2 Opposite Low Blean Farm there is a high ladder stile leading to the lake side path signed "FP Stalling Busk 1 ¼ miles". Walk in single file through the pastures with a mixture of gates and stiles through each boundary wall. Semer Water is just on the right with Green Scar Crag overlooking the lake on the far shore.

Stalling Busk Old Church dates from around 1722. In its 200 years of use it served as the burial place for some 750 local people. Built on the site of an earlier church it fell into disuse when the new Church of St Matthew was built up in the village itself in 1909.

Stalling Busk Old Church

Cross over a stile at a field barn and the lakeshore path proper is reached. The head of Semer Water is passed and the path continues straight on through the fields heading towards

Raydale. The path rises barely 50 feet above the valley bottom and continues passing the odd hawthorn tree along the way. The ruins of Stalling Busk Old Church with its double arches are passed on the right.

3 Just past the church and through a gate stile the path forks; take the lower right hand fork signed to Marsett. Route finding is simple on the clear green path through the meadows passing field barns and through stiles one of which is particularly narrow! The path drops to the valley floor and proceeds towards some trees, with a wall on the right. A stream is crossed over a metal footbridge where an unsurfaced lane is joined; follow this to the right towards Marsett. Barely a hundred yards further along a second stream is crossed either by ford or footbridge. Now simply follow the unsurfaced lane along Raydale to the village of Marsett.

(4) At Marsett follow the river-bank to join the road at a red phone box beside Marsett Bridge. Cross the bridge over Marsett Beck and follow the road for 10 yards where an unsurfaced walled lane turns off to the left heading up the hillside signed "FP Burtersett 2miles and Hawes 3 miles". The walled lane gently rises up the hillside above Marsett. For a low level alternative just follow the road all the way back to the start.

(5) At a metal gate on the right with an adjacent wooden stile a footpath waymarker arrow points the way over the stile to go up the green path straight up the hillside. This is a fairly stiff climb straight up to the ridge above. The way is through four field lengths straight up the hillside. As height is gained the retrospective views down onto Marsett, Semer Water and into Raydale improve as height is gained. Keep the

Addlebrough

Meadows on the way to Marsett

drystone wall to the left for the first three enclosures before climbing a giant ladder stile into the last field where the path continues rising. The rate of ascent decreases nearing the crest of the ridge.

6 Just below a limestone scar on the left a green track is crossed, this is the path across the top. Turn right to walk along the top of the ridge with the distinctive shape of Addlebrough on the horizon. The green track continues gently rising to a gate in the wall crossing the felltop.

Continue along the green track. The village of Stalling Busk clings to the hillside on the opposite side of the valley. After a final rise the track goes over the summit of the hill at 1670' where the views open out to the west along Wensleydale. Continue on the track through another gated wall. Just past the gate the path forks; take the right hand path heading down towards Semer Water. Height is lost on a well built path around the front of the hill.

7 Follow the path down through a couple more fields before it reaches the surfaced road, where all that's required is to walk down the road back to the start point. At the road junction at the outskirts of Countersett go straight across and down the road to the car park.

6 Mill Gill Falls from Askrigg

Delightful woodland walk to impressive falls

The popular village of Askrigg is the start point for this beckside walk. Askrigg's name is Norse in origin meaning "the ridge where ash trees grow" and the area still has its fair share of ash trees. The old market square retains its cobbles and marketcross from 1830 together with a stone pump and an iron bull ring set into the cobbles. The walk visits the single spout of Mill Gill Force

Level:

Length: 3 miles (5km)

Ascent: 500 feet (150m)

Terrain: Woodland paths returning along an unsurfaced lane

Park and Start: Centre of Askrigg GR 948 910

Info: Toilets and refreshments in Askrigg

with the additional possibility to visit Whitfield Gill Force which is further upstream. Whilst Mill Gill Force can safely be seen in its full glory, Whitfield Gill Force which is prominently marked on OS maps is barely visible through the trees and is hardly worth making the additional effort.

St Oswald's, Askrigg

and keep following the signs for "Mill Gill Force". Cross the gill over a narrow footbridge and simply follow the path at the edge of the trees now on the left bank of the gill. The path climbs high above the tree lined gill along the edge of the wood with fields just over the wall on the left.

(1) Park on the cobbled setts by the church in the middle of Askrigg by the old market cross. Walk down the lane to the right of the church signed "Footpath to Mill Gill Foss". Follow the road through the back of the village. Towards the end of the village the first set of Askrigg's old mill buildings appears on the left.

(2) As the end of the village is reached and the road loses its surface a flagged path through the meadows heads off through a gate on the right signposted "Mill Gill Force". The flagged path leads through the hay meadow towards the gill. Pass a second mill and walk beneath the old mill race around the back of the mill

Mill building, Askrigg

Footbridge over Mill Gill

(3) Where the path forks and take the detour down to the right to visit "Mill Gill Falls only". The path drops down through the trees to impressive Mill Gill Force. Having visited the falls retrace the path back up the valley side to rejoin the main path and continue upstream by taking the right hand fork towards Whitfield Gill. You may spot a minor path to the right which leads to an impressive square lime kiln just 20 yards along. Heading upstream the path pops out of the woods to follow a field boundary wall. The path drops back through the wall and continue heading left signed Whitfield Gill up the left bank of the stream. Ignore the path heading over the gill and back to Askrigg at this point. Keep heading upstream following the signs to Whitfield Gill.

Mill Gill Force

(4) Where the path forks the main route now heads down to the right to "Askrigg via Low Straits". To take a look at Whitfield Force take the left fork to continue up the valley to try and get a glimpse of Whitfield Force through the trees — this proves to be almost impossible in the summer with leaves on the trees. Continuing on the main route the path drops down the valley side to pass some minor falls. The path crosses the beck over a narrow footbridge and then proceeds to rise up the opposite bank through the trees.

(5) The path emerges onto the top of the walled Low Strait Lane where its downhill all the way back to Askrigg barely a mile away. Follow the walled lane down the hillside with open views across

Wensleydale. Pass a track on the right down to Leas House Farm and continue down Low Strait Lane with the unmistakeable shape of Addlebrough on the right across the dale. The track continues losing height and fords the tree-lined Askrigg Beck.

6 Leave the lane by a giant ash tree through a wall stile where a fingerpost "FP Askrigg ½ mile" points the way to the right past a field barn. Keep to the field edge straight on down towards Askrigg. Before long the tower of Askrigg church comes into view straight ahead. At the narrow bottom of the field go over the stile where a fingerpost points to the front left onto a farm track. Follow the track and then the stream to emerge through the back of some cottages onto a narrow lane in Askrigg. Turn right and in 20 yards right again onto the main road through the village to walk back to the start.

St Oswald's Church is the largest church in Wensleydale. The church built in 1466 in the Perpendicular style has an impressive tower. Restoration in the 1880s included the installation of a new stained glass east window in memory of George Winn who drowned crossing the Aysgarth Ford.

Barn on Low Strait Lane

Low Strait Lane

7 Around Addlebrough

A long circuit around Wensleydale's most distinctive hill

At some 500 feet lower than Wether Hill, nevertheless Addlebrough dominates the scene along the middle of Wensleydale. With its distinctive shape the top of the hill is surrounded by a ring of limestone crags. The summit of the hill is a scheduled ancient monument to protect a set of pre-historic cup and ring stone marks. Whilst access to the top of the hill has recently been made possible

Level: ❤ ❤
Length: 6 miles (9.5km)
Ascent: 700 feet (210m)
Terrain: Steady incline on clear paths to the high point
Park and Start: Thornton Rust GR972 888
Info: No facilities on route

by the addition of a permissive path from the road by agreement from the landowner (the National Trust) this walk avoids the summit and circles below the summit scars. The route gives outstanding views of three of the other walks in this collection, namely walks 4,5,6.

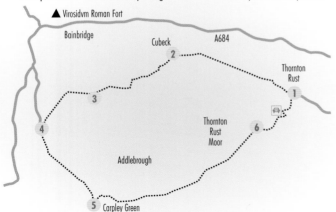

▲ Virosidvm Roman Fort

Bainbridge

Cubeck

A684

2

Thornton Rust

1

3

Thornton Rust Moor

6

4

Addlebrough

5 Carpley Green

Approaching Cubeck

1 Start from the Village
Institute building in Thornton
Rust. Parking is available just up the
lane opposite the Village Institute.
The walk starts with just over a mile
of road walking along the quiet lane
through the village heading west

towards the hamlet of Cubeck. The
walled grounds of Thornton Lodge are
passed on the left. The roadsides are
an array of wild flowers in the summer. This is a nice easy start to the
walk along this narrow quiet lane.
The road drops down as it approaches
the hamlet of Cubeck.

2 As the road swings sharply
round to the right continue
straight on into Cubeck following the
sign "Public Bridleway Carpley Green
Road 1½ mile" which points up an
unsurfaced lane through a gate beside
a field barn. The track immediately
starts to rise up the hillside towards
the yet unseen Addlebrough. The track

*Thornton Rust is a linear
village running along a
limestone "bench" above
Wensleydale. Many of the
buildings date from the
seventeenth to nineteenth
centuries. The principal
exception being the Village
Institute which was built as
a memorial to the fallen of
the First World War in 1924.*

Looking across to Askrigg

levels off for a few short yards and then continues through the left of a pair of gates and then continues to rise up the hillside with a wall now on the right hand side. As the path flattens out again there is a view across the valley to Askrigg and in fact the whole of Walk 6 can be seen. The path swings around to the left heading straight for Addlebrough and continues to gently rise. The flat table-topped Addlebrough can now be clearly seen ahead with a limestone scar around its western face.

Go through a gap in the wall, with Addlebrough straight ahead. The path splits three ways so take the right hand path aiming for the gap through the next wall. Through the next gate hole, and the path now forks, both paths lead to the same point across the next field but the right of way is the thinner left hand path across the moorland.

3 Both paths meet up at a gate almost in line with the end of Addlebrough and after 10 yards the path forks again. Whilst the OS map shows the bridleway making its way across country to the left the far easier path to follow is the right hand path which tracks around following the wall all the way to join Carpley Green Road above Semer Water.

Addlebrough

4 The green path arrives at a gate onto Carpley Green Road where the view now opens out straight down below onto Semer Water. In fact you can see most of Walks 4 and 5 from this point. Turn left to walk along the quiet enclosed lane heading to Carpley Green. The road winds its way around the back of Addlebrough.

5 Just before reaching Carpley Green Farm a fingerpost points through a gate to the left "Bridleway Thornton Rust 2¼". A faint path rises through the field towards Addlebrough with a wall on the right. At the top of the field go through a wooden gate and a green path veers off to the front left on a slightly raised bank above the moorland and then proceeds around the southern slopes of Addlebrough. The clear path through the long-grassed moorland goes around the hinterland of Addlebrough. Pass through a gate in a wall and continue heading back to Thornton Rust across Thornton Rust Moor. The wide path proceeds across

Across the valley from Carpley Green Road

the open moorland with open views along Wensleydale; Castle Bolton is ever prominent. The path passes through another gate to leave the moorland and enters the enclosures above Thornton Rust.

6 The path meets up with a farm track in front of a wall; turn to the right and simply follow the track down the hillside into Thornton Rust and back to the start.

8 Aysgarth Falls

A walk around Wensleydale's best known falls

Aysgarth Falls is one of the most popular locations in the Yorkshire Dales National Park. The falls have attracted visitors for over 200 years including the poet William Wordsworth and his new wife Mary, accompanied by his ever present sister Dorothy, who visited the day after their marriage in 1802. The artist JMW Turner visited Aysgarth Falls on

Level:

Length: 2¾ miles (4.5km)

Ascent: 250 feet (75m)

Terrain: Well laid paths, unsurfaced lanes and field paths

Park and Start: Aysgarth Falls National Park Centre

Info: Toilets and refreshments available at the start

his way to Hardraw on his 1816 trip. The falls themselves are made up of three distinctive waterfalls: the Upper Falls above the bridge, the Middle Falls beside Freeholders Wood and the Lower Falls which are the highest of the three falls and best seen after rain when the river is full.

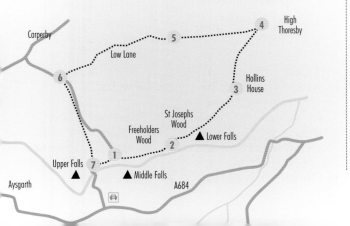

1 Start from the YDNP Car Park in Aysgarth. Leave the car park heading back to the road signed to the Middle and Lower Falls. Turn right for 20 yards down the road and take care as you cross the road to enter Freeholders Wood and Riddings Field Nature Reserve. Take the well laid path following the sign "FP Lower and Middle Falls" where the sounds of the crashing water can be heard. The path diverts almost immediately with a waymarker pointing to visit the Middle Falls. Heed the warning signs to stay within the confines of the view-ing platform and then head back up to the main trail through the coppiced woodland towards the Lower Falls. Passing through a gate Freeholders Wood is left behind and the sounds of the Lower Falls can be heard down on the right.

Heed the warning!

2 Follow the signs directing you to the Lower Falls viewing platform. This takes you on a well signed and clearly defined loop through the trees to visit the Lower Falls before returning back to the main path. Turn right along the main path for barely 20 yards where a Walkers Sign points to a green path veering off to the left signed to "Castle Bolton and Redmire". The meadows contain a rich variety of wild flowers in the spring and early summer. A gate leads through the wall exiting St Josephs Wood up through the meadows to Hollins Farm which can be seen ahead and then on towards Castle Bolton. Follow the wide green path through the meadows. As the path gets further away from the river and gently rises the views open out across and down the dale.

Lower Falls

3 The path passes between the collection of buildings at Hollins Farm and the way continues on an unsurfaced farm track. The imposing sight of Bolton Castle appears ahead and a fingerpost signed "Footpath" shows the way veering off to the right away from the farm track heading towards Castle Bolton. Go through one field and then over a wall stile signed to "Castle Bolton" where a green path heads straight across the next field.

4 Approaching a stile through the wall at the end of the field to Thoresby Farm turn left staying inside the field boundary and walk beside the drystone wall through a gate and then underneath one of the

"…over a wall stile signed to Castle Bolton"

Thoresby Farm and Castle Bolton

The bridge across the Ure
at Aysgarth has existed
for centuries. The 1539
packhorse bridge was the
only crossing of the river
between Wensley and
Bainbridge. A century later
it was in ruins. The repaired
bridge was finally widened
to its current size in 1788
at a cost of £420.

bridges of the disused Wensleydale Railway. Continue straight on following the line of the wall on the right through another gate and past a corrugated iron barn. Past a second barn and through the gate at the end of the field to arrive at a surfaced lane.

(5) Continue straight on along the quiet narrow Low Lane for just over half a mile. The village of Carperby can be seen across the fields on the right, simply keep walk along the lane to arrive at the Aysgarth to Carperby road.

(6) Turn left to walk down the road for 20 yards where a fingerpost on the right hand side of the road points the way through the fields down to Aysgarth and the Upper Falls. Go through the narrow wall stile at the end of the first field and follow the fingerpost pointing down the second field. Start to veer to the right

through Bear Park, to arrive at a lonely gatestile at the bottom of the field and then enter the trees where an iron kissing gate gives entry into the woods above the car park. Cross back over the abandoned railway and drop back down to the car park.

(7) Turn right for the short walk along the path to visit the Upper Falls. Follow the well signed path down the hill to visit the third flight of Aysgarth Falls.

Walking across the fields

Surging waters

9 Castle Bolton to Carperby

A walk through the fields between Castle Bolton and Carperby

The impressive medieval stronghold of Bolton Castle dominates the north side of central Wensleydale and can be seen from a number of the walks in this collection. Dating from 1399, the castle was built by Sir Richard le Scrope, Lord Chancellor of England to Richard II. The castle has never been sold and remains in the private ownership of Lord Bolton, Sir

Level:
Length: 4 ¾ miles (7.6km)
Ascent: 450 feet (135m)
Terrain: Gently undulating unsurfaced lane and field paths
Park and Start: Car Park at Bolton Castle GR 033 918
Info: Toilets at start, refreshments from The Wheatsheaf in Carperby www.boltoncastle.co.uk

Richard le Scrope's direct descendant. The Scropes remained loyal to King Charles during the Civil War. The East Curtain wall was thrown down following a successful six month siege by Parliamentary troops in 1645.

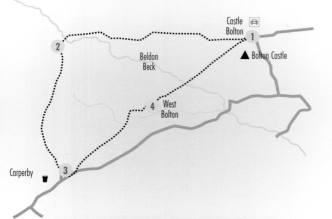

Bolton Castle

Limestone Scar above Carperby

(1) Start from the National Park Car Park at the top of Castle Bolton village just behind the castle itself. Leave the car park and turn right onto the lane in front of the car park signed "FP Aysgarth 3 miles". It's straight forward and easy walking along the farm track heading up the valley towards Carperby with limestone scars on the horizon and an extensive view up the dale. The track swings up to the right and gently rises through a field to pass a stand of trees, an old sheepwash and a collection of three modern wooden barns. The track goes through a gate in the wall and continues signed to Carperby. The track passes through a new plantation of rowan trees and then back through the wall and continues as a green track. After crossing a stream or dry beck go through a gate where a sign directs you to "Carperby 1 ½ mile" continuing across the open moors.

The railway line running along the length of Wensleydale was built by the North Eastern Railway Company in the 1870s. The line was immediately popular bringing both trade and tourism into the dale. The advent of the bus and motor car sent the railway into decline and the line was eventually closed in 1964.

"...the path gently descends besides a wall to Carperby"

2 The track now turns and starts to head back towards the valley. Through another gate and the track forks; take the lower left hand fork which is signed down to Carperby now only ¾ mile. The path starts to drop down to Carperby and the view down the dale opens out back to Castle Bolton. The path gently descends besides a wall to join an unsurfaced lane for the last ½ mile into Carperby.

3 The lane arrives at the back of Carperby where the road forks: either will take you onto the main road through the village. Arriving at the main road through Carperby, turn left to continue the journey or alternatively turn right to visit The Wheatsheaf before resuming

The lane into Carperby

the walk back to Castle Bolton. Passing the last farm in the village on the left a wall stile goes onto a path which is signed "Castle Bolton 1¾ mile". The return route is a fairly straight line gently rising through the fields to Castle Bolton. The path goes along the field edge around the back of the farm and then onto an unsurfaced farm track gently rising up to the right. The lane ends at a gate into a field with a restored field barn where the path goes in straight line across the fields through various walled enclosures to West Bolton Plantation. Crossing a steam in a depression the path continues around the top end of West Bolton Plantation of mixed woodland where another sign points to Castle Bolton, initially heading towards West Bolton Farm.

Castle Bolton to Carperby

Twisted hawthorn on the top lane

(4) The route passes in front of West Bolton Farm and continues through the fields heading for the imposing sight of Castle Bolton just under a mile away. The way proceeds over a wall stile at the top left hand corner of the first field past the farm and then crosses Bolden Beck over a narrow footbridge before continuing on short cropped grass to the castle. The path gently rises crossing wooden stiles over fences for the final stretch up to the trees at the start point. At the top of the last field the path meets the outbound track and all that remains is to walk back to the start.

"What are you looking at?"

10 Redmire Force from West Witton

Visit the Wensleydale's last major set of falls

This last walk in the book is to the second set of falls along the Ure: Redmire Force. Often described as a mini Aysgarth Falls due to having three steps, in fact Redmire Force has its own distinctive character and is well worth a visit in its own right. The walk makes its way down to the banks of the Ure from the village of West Witton along an ancient

Level:
Length: 4½ miles (7.2km)
Ascent: 300 feet (90m)
Terrain: Riverbank paths and gently undulating walled lanes
Park and Start: Roadside in middle of West Witton GR 060 884
Info: Refreshments from Fox and Hounds pub and The Wensleydale Heiffer seventeenth-century inn.

enclosed lane before following the course of the Ure for nearly 2 miles to reach the falls. If you are lucky you may even get to hear and see one of the steam trains running on the re-opened Wensleydale Railway on the opposite bank.

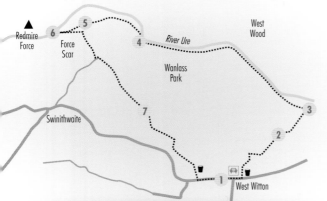

West Witton from Back Lane

Bull calf in the fields

1 Park along the roadside anywhere safe through the centre of the village. Walk along the road to the eastern end of the village. Just past the Old Vicarage and opposite a red pillar box before a bus stop a narrow lane doubles back on itself down to the left. After 20 yards a narrow walled lane goes to the right signed "Footpath"; this is the start of Back Lane heading down to the River Ure. The ancient lane zig zags down towards the river.

2 The lane comes to an end at the entrance to a field. Go through the narrow wall stile to enter the field and continue walking through the field keeping the drystone wall to your left. It's pathless through this large field; keep just walking down towards the Ure keeping the wall close on the left hand side. The imposing sight of Bolton Hall comes into view on the opposite bank of the river.

River Ure

3 As the wall turns away to the left, the OS maps show the right of way heading away to the right, however a narrow path on the ground continues to head down to the left towards an iron gate through the wall towards the bottom of the field, where the path crosses over a stream to arrive at a three-pointed walkers signpost.

Follow the fingerpost to "Hestholme Bridge for West Burton and Aysgarth"

which is the narrow trod beside the stream down to the river. Cross a stile over a fence to pick up the riverside path heading upstream towards Redmire Force. Castle Bolton appears on the hillside in the distance. The Ure splits as it passes either side of the long thin Batt Island. Just below High Wanlass Farm, keep to the path which hugs the riverbank.

4 As the Ure turns away from the path at a high tree-covered bank follow the path down the bank and cross the meadowland heading straight towards Castle Bolton on the horizon. The path cuts the corner of the bend in the river and makes for a drystone wall. The path continues now beside the wall with the trees which line the banks of a backwater of the Ure below on the right over the wall.

Bolton Hall on the opposite bank of the Ure is the private home of Lord and Lady Bolton, the owners of Castle Bolton. The hall was completed in 1675 by the first Duke of Bolton, Charles Paulett and his wife Mary.

Redmire Force from West Witton

River Ure

5 After passing along the edge of a large green hillocky field the path arrives at a giant ladder stile over the wall. The track which marks the start of the return route is joined on the other side of the wall. But it would be a shame to miss Redmire Force having got so close, so to make the detour to visit the falls, go straight on through the next field keeping the wall on your right. The sound of the falls gets louder the nearer you approach to the as yet unseen falls. At the far corner of the field a wooden gate goes through the wall signed "Footpath" on a clear path through the tress heading to the falls. Redmire Force is a triple decker set of falls over which the Ure pairs on its way down the dale.

6 Having visited the falls retrace your steps back to the track at the ladder stile and then follow the track up the meadows away from the river back up towards West Witton. The track goes through two fields and at the end of the second field approaching a wood take the left hand gate of the two gates to follow the footpath up through the field to the left of the plantation of trees signed "Bridleway". Reaching the top of the trees aim for the top left hand corner of this next large field where a narrow gate leads into the next field and a Bridleway marker shows the way forward keeping to the left hand edge of the second field.

Shallows on the Ure

Redmire Force from West Witton

7 At the top left hand corner the beginning of an enclosed lane is reached through a wooden gate and again signed "Bridleway". Walk up the narrow enclosed lane heading towards the noisy road. As the green lane approaches the road, pass through an iron gate and as the lane turns to the right a walkers' gate goes through the wall on the left to begin a path through the pastures at the back of the village avoiding the road signed "FP West Witton ¼". Go straight across the first field through the gap in the wall. Rise diagonally through the second field aiming for the top right hand corner and a wooden gate which enters a fenced path into the back of West Witton. Emerge onto the main road and walk back to the waiting car.

Blokes with Balls

Blokes with Balls

Jeremy Clay

CONTENTS

INTRODUCTION

The match was already in full swing when the Elland Road tannoy crackled into life with an urgent message for a Leeds fan in the crowd.

"Please hurry to the Bradford Royal Infirmary," the announcer said, with the too-jolly tone of a local radio DJ introducing yet another underwhelming prize draw: "your wife is having a baby."

Both sets of supporters mustered something approaching a congratulatory cheer, then fixed their concentration straight back on the game.

Forty minutes later, the announcer was back with the same message, delivered with a more plaintive tone.

The third, and by now faintly disapproving plea came just before the final whistle, to a roar of disbelieving guffaws from the terraces.

The mother of his soon-to-be newborn child may have been tumbling through the nine circles of hell in the maternity unit, but dad … well, y'know he was busy too.

This possibly apocryphal bloke isn't in this book. If you're skim-reading this in Waterstones and like the sound of him, perhaps you should just pop it back on the shelves. He doesn't figure again. We couldn't find him you see – perhaps after finally showing his face he never survived the rightful wrath of his missus.

But he's here in spirit, just like the bridegroom who dashed from his wedding reception to catch a QPR game, the Spurs fan who flies back from Boston for home games and the rather curious chap who keeps a neatly-indexed store of tapes of his team's manager's post-game radio interviews.

It takes all sorts, or so they say. But in this book, it just takes these sorts.

THE HEART OF THE MATTER

Stick on the kettle, pull up a seat, let me tell you a second-hand story.

Once upon a time – well, last year, to be exact - there was a man called Don Cole. Perhaps there still is, though for reasons which will soon become plain, that's by no means guaranteed.

Don was a fan of University of Alabama's football team who followed his idols home and away. Nothing too surprising in that, you might think. And you'd be right, if it wasn't for the fact that his doctor removed his name from the heart transplant waiting list every time he strayed more than two hours away from the hospital in Nashville.

"If I can't go to Alabama football games what's the point in living?" he reasons in Rammer Jammer Yellow Hammer, Warren St. John's portrait of life among the Alabama hardcore.

Now it might sound to some like Don should be making inquiries about a place on the brain transplant waiting list too, but one in four football fans in England know just how he feels. Or felt, possibly.

A survey for internet search engine Yahoo found 28 per cent of supporters would rather miss a vital operation than the first game of the season.

It doesn't end there: one in six would skip their own wedding if it was a straight choice between their big day or the big match.

Meanwhile, a study in the USA discovered an alarmingly high number of American sports fans would merrily bump off a rival team's star player if they knew they could get away with it.

And the lesson of all this? Simple: Don't get engaged to one-in-six football fans, and wear a stab-proof vest in the States if you're nifty at basketball.

Actually, no, there's another lesson: the love of your team, like a love of your country, can sometimes get a little out of hand.

Not for everyone, naturally. Fans aren't the uniform herd of cash cows they appear to be from the directors' box.

Take a single stand in a single stadium on match day and you'll find enough different shades of support to make you wonder if perhaps we should commandeer a few spare Eskimo words for snow to describe them all.

There, at the back, clutching the free tickets they got from work are the sort-of supporters, men with little more than a notional attachment to the club, which usually only emerges in awkward conversations with the plumber.

There, to the left and right, are the casual fans, who treat the fixture list like a menu, cherry-picking the games that tickle their fancy between trips to the cinema, the gardening centre and IKEA.

And here, there and everywhere are the regulars, who turn up week in, week out, no matter how dire the performances.

But it's the obsessives down the front that concern us here; the fanatics, the ultras, the anoraks and self-confessed sad-sacks. The men who have forgotten exactly where they end and their club begins. The kind of blokes whose thoughts turn to their teams during sex; not as a safeguard against premature ejaculation but merely because they can't keep their mind off the club for long.

A HASTILY-RESEARCHED HISTORY LESSON

From the very earliest times mankind has found distraction in games like wrestling, archery and other equally gimpy pursuits.

The ancient Egyptians were partial to the javelin and high jump. The ancient Greeks loved a bit of discus and a nice chariot race. And the Chinese are credited with the earliest form of footy, a game called Tsu Chu which involved kicking a leather ball through a hole in a piece of silk cloth strung between two 30 foot poles. (Try making those goalposts with jumpers.)

So with sport safely invented, all that was then needed were some spectators. They can't have been far behind. A rudimentary knowledge of human nature tells us that there's always somebody ready to watch any old rubbish.

And once you've got a few fans, you'll get one who takes it a bit too far.

Enter Han Dynasty Emperor Wudi, who was surely one of the first recorded sporting obsessives. He was so devoted to Tsu Chu he ordered that all the best players move to the capital so he could watch them play. An early Roman Abramovich, then.

But Wudi isn't the only figure in history to lose the plot because of sport.

Think for a moment of Francis Drake, who famously finished his bowls match on Plymouth Hoe while the Spanish Armada lurked menacingly on the horizon.

For centuries that's been held up as a benchmark for plucky Britishness, a prime example of our chap keeping a cool-head just before sticking it to Johnny Foreigner.

But perhaps there's another reason. Maybe Drake was just completely engrossed in the game.

And imagine what he'd be like if he'd had a proper sport to follow. If the Spanish assembled off the south coast today, you'd probably find him shirtless at Home Park, with a Plymouth tattoo across his droopy manmaries and his son Argyle by his side, studiously ignoring the text message from a military underling reading: Spnrds R Here :-(

PAY ATTENTION, HERE'S THE SOCIAL SCIENCE

One word, three letters: Why?

Why devote your life to a team that rewards your undying love by mugging you at the turnstiles, fleecing you in the club shop, half-poisoning you at the food bar and then sending you home with a stress headache every other week?

If anyone knows, it's Northumbria University psychologist Dr Sandy Wolfson, who's been studying obsessive football fans since Euro 96.

First the good news: "Being a football supporter is basically psychologically healthy," she says.

Now the bad: There are "amazing similarities" between football fans and those bi-focalled pariahs of popular culture, the much-lampooned Trekkies.

Yikes.

"It's not a theory that's popular with either party, but they have so much in common," says Dr Wolfson. "It's the same behaviour. The collecting, the idolising of the stars, the dutiful going to conventions, the memorising of information."

"Star Trek fans know what you are talking about when you mention Season 3 Episode 4, and football fans know exactly what you mean when you talk about that penalty miss in 1997.

"Star Trek fans may be characterised as intellectual nerds and football fans as yobs but there are so many parallels between the two."

Lumme: let's quickly return to the good news.

"Sport – and none more than football – lets people exercise their intellect," says Dr Wolfson.

"Anybody can watch a game and have an opinion about what went right and what went wrong, whether the manager made the correct choice of tactics and whether the ref was awful or not.

"Plus you can shout, swear and scream in public. There are not many areas of modern life you can do that. It's very cathartic.

"And people enjoy feeling part of a larger group. This drive to be part of a wider group dates back to primitive times and it's innate in humans."

So there you go: the stands from Highbury and Old Trafford to Oakwell and the New Den are full of people indulging their inner caveman. Particularly at the New Den.

But why are some people merely fans and others fanatics?

"There are individual differences, of course," says Dr Wolfson. "You get people who tend to take things to the extreme; people with addictive personalities latch onto things that absorb them."

That's the verdict of the shrink. But let's get it from the horse's mouth: how do the blokes in this book explain their devotion to their teams?

"Stockport County mean everything to me," says Ian Lancashire. "Absolutely everything."

"If I woke up and thought I can't be arsed with this, I wouldn't go anymore," says Leeds

United zealot Gary Edwards. "It hasn't happened yet."

"Some people call me stupid," says Norman Windram, who's been following Manchester United for 78 years. "But it's my enjoyment in life. I'd sooner go and watch United than sit all day in the pub, boozing."

"It's just one of those daft things," says Jim McGuinness, who saves all year to spend his holiday entitlement at cricket Test matches abroad, dressed as Sylvester the Cat. "I do it for a laugh."

MEN ONLY
A good man may be hard to find, but an obsessive one? Well, they're all around you.

Women get engrossed by sport too, says Dr Wolfson, who happily admits to scheduling her meetings and conferences around all the Newcastle United fixtures. But there can't be too many female fans that go to the game then dash home to plunge themselves back into their warm, safe mini-world of chronologically-filed programmes and well-thumbed copies of the Rothman's Yearbook. If there are, I haven't heard of them.

Despite the enormous strides made in gender equality, a life-distorting fixation with sport is still chiefly a male malaise.

So women hover in the margins of these stories.

Sometimes they're the long-suffering other-halves who deal with the excesses of their menfolk with a roll of the eyes and a world-weary sigh.

Sometimes they're the women who happily feed the addiction ("my wife has been ensnared in my web," says 1970/71 season obsessive Bob Dunning. "She'll go out to charity shops and come back with a Stan Bowles autobiography for me.")

And sometimes they're the wives who've simply had enough, and walked out.

Divorce was a word that figured disproportionately regularly during the conversations with these men. Make of that what you will.

"I've had three wives," says Stockport County die-hard Ian Lancashire. "That probably tells you all you need to know."

THE INEVITABLE TOP 10

There are 36 stories in this book. Enough men to have an overcrowded kickabout up the park. And all of them, in one way or another, have an addiction.

It won't leave them shuddering in urine-soaked doorways; it won't make them rob their own grannies and it won't force them to move to Hastings and sit for hours on the seafront with hellzapoppin eyes, but an addiction is an addiction all the same, whether it's to a team, a sport or a class A drug.

But we shouldn't forget that sport does strange things to people. And to get these men in a little context, let's satisfy that other peculiarly male trait - a love of lists – with a randomly-selected Top 10 of fans' odd behaviour.

1. A man in the Maldives was chucked in prison for practising black magic to skew the score of a football match.

Abdullah Haleelu jinxed a rival team in a ritual that culminated in him writing players' names on coconut shells. And he got the result he was after: his team went on to win the final game of the season.

Alas, Abdullah was unlicensed to perform the curse, so off to chokey he went.

2. Fans of a lowly Croatian team collected potatoes to keep the club's promotion drive on course.

When the cash-strapped Nedeljanec FC fell into the red, the supporters came to the rescue by donating six tonnes of spuds to sell and raise funds to bankroll the club through the rest of the season.

3. They know how to celebrate a big win in Detroit: Hockey fans of the Red Wings hurl, erm, octopi on to the ice in a surreal tradition dating back to the early 1950s. The largest octopus ever thrown, fact fans, was a 50 pounder in 1996.

4. A gaggle of Germans who found themselves without a team to support when their club went bust marketed themselves as rent-a-fans in return for beer and sausages.

The SC Goettingen 05 supporters pledged to chant and cheer any club in need of a little lift, for the price of hotdogs and lager.

5. When the talismatic England goalkeeper Gordon Banks lost an eye in a car crash in 1972, the football world was stunned.

Step forward a Leicester mum-of-four with a startlingly selfless offer of assistance. "The news about the accident has been such a shock," she told the Leicester Mercury. "I wear glasses but if it will be any help he can have one of my eyes."

6. A Brazilian football fan tied himself to a tree in a one-man demonstration of anger against his club's wretched form.

Corinthians nut Roberto (have the Brazilians entirely done away with surnames?) chomped on bananas and hurled the skins at the nearby stadium while demanding changes to the team line-up and tactics. Eventually he ran out, which was kind of apt for such a fruitless protest.

7. Five Chelsea fans were bound over to keep the peace after throwing sticks of celery at each other during a FA Cup semi-final.

"It was good natured and the celery did not cause any injury or damages," conceded the prosecution.

8. A Boca Juniors fan in Buenos Aires who spent his life as tradition demands, hating River Plate, asked to be wrapped in his rivals' flag on his deathbed. Why? So he could celebrate, with his last breath, the death of 'one of them'. Nice.

9. There seems to be something in the water in Alabama. Freeman and Betty Reese skipped their own daughter's wedding because it coincided with the University of Alabama's clash with Tennessee. The bride could take some solace in the fact her parents turned up in time for the reception.

10. A Hereford fan cancelled his wedding after a moment of epiphany mid-way through his stag-do. It wasn't a sudden loss of love for his bride-to-be, he just realised the day the happy couple had arranged to get hitched clashed with his team's FA Cup clash at Aylesbury.

Jeremy Clay

HALLOWED BE THY GAME

"SO WHAT *WOULD* JESUS SAY TO SAM ALLARDYCE?"

We know what He said on the cross. We know what He said in the wilderness. And we've got a pretty good idea what He'll say to Maradona when he finally gets to have a quiet word over that Hand of God nonsense. But what would Jesus say to Sam Allardyce?

In 2,000 years of theology, that's not a question that's cropped up a great deal. But as Bolton faced the drop at the business end of the 2002/03 season, it was nagging away at ticket holder Canon Roger. So he turned it into a sermon. And decorated his church to represent the Reebok Stadium. And handed out half-time oranges to the congregation. And asked a man who looked a little like Sam to shout team tactics from the pews.

"We invited Sam too," says Roger, with the ghost of a sigh. "But we got a letter back saying it was the last day of the season and he had a match to go to."

So what *would* Jesus say to Sam Allardyce? "He'd say 'I know how you feel. Bolton are letting in lots of goals. Then he'd speak of the dreams Sam has for his team and the dreams God has for us." Bolton, by the way, survived. Draw your own conclusions.

A BRIEF HISTORY OF POSH PANTS

The man on the phone is describing his underwear. "They're blue, white and black briefs," he says, in the lascivious tones of someone used to telling strangers about his Ys. "And they're very tight. But I'm afraid they've seen better days," he adds, a note of rude reality creeping in. "In fact they ride up a little."

This might sound like a catastrophically-misdialled 0898 chat line, but it's only John talking about his lucky pants, the humble chads that bring good fortune to Peterborough United near enough everytime he pulls them on. They came in a pack of three; from BHS, probably. John's forgotten where and when when he bought them. But seventy times he's strolled into London Road sporting his magic Ups; and sixty five times he's walked out a winner.

"It's an incredible record," John says. Indeed it is. And he works hard to maintain it. Here's the method: John's law firm sponsors a game. He dons his undies, heads for the tunnel, and goes out onto the pitch. Then – and only then – he touches the matchball, while the ref's still holding it.

It's like a kecks hex: and near-as-dammit spells victory for the Posh. But there's only so much these tatty smalls can do. "I wore them on The Weakest Link," says John, ruefully. "I was the fourth one voted off."

"THEY'RE A BIT MANKY REALLY. AND THEY'RE NOT VERY COMFORTABLE."

A LOAN AGAIN, NATURALLY

"IT'S THE FLAG OF SHAME."

The Hole In The Wall gang, that's what they called themselves: five lads named after the pub where they met up. But the nickname might just as easily have come from a cashpoint; the one they used to buy a stay of execution for the ailing love of their lives.

Devoted fans are two a penny in sport. But Paul and his mates were like gold dust to the London Broncos – when the rugby league team was on the verge of extinction they drained their bank accounts to keep it alive.

"It was 1993," he says. "We were really, really crap and completely broke. The club went into administration and we had a week to pay the players' wages. So I took out a student loan for £1,300. It was the most I could get. My dad still doesn't know I did it. I suppose he will now…" 'Fraid so Paul.

In his living room in Middlesbrough ("I moved up here for work", he explains, "it's 254.8 miles from the Broncos' ground"), Paul waves the tatty old keepsake of his team's one and only trip to Wembley. "It's the Flag of Shame", he says. "Every game I take it to we lose. Guaranteed." So why take it? "Yeah", he says, after a short pause. "You'd think I'd have thought of that by now, wouldn't you?"

POMPEY AND CIRCUMSTANCE

It's getting a little tricky to pick out a single Portsmouth tattoo amid the 50 or so jostling for space on John's arms, chest and Lord knows what else.

But somewhere on that ever-increasing skin-gallery there's one that pretty much sums up the only heavily-tattooed antiquarian bookseller in Britain. It's a sketch of a man having sex with a coconut. Underneath it says I'm Nuts About Pompey. (Or at least it would if the tattooist had taken a firmer line on swearing. Use your imagination for the full uncensored wording.)

And if all those tattoos aren't enough of a clue to John's mindset, then a glance at his credit card should do the trick. John Anthony Portsmouth Football Club, it reads, and has done since he changed his name by deed poll 15 years ago.

"It's on my cards, my passport, everything," he says, with a smile that reveals PFC picked out in gold on his teeth. "My signature is a scrawl, but I make sure the PFC is readable. Anything to do with Pompey and I go OTT."

There is, naturally, a downside to his obsession. "It can be a bit of an obstacle," he concedes. "When it comes to chatting up girls they think I'm like this seven days a week. It is a bit frustrating."

"I LIVE AND BREATHE POMPEY."

TO ELLAND BACK

"IT'S LIKE CHRISTMAS MORNING FOR ME EVERY TIME I GO AND SEE LEEDS."

He's never done the maths; never sat down with a calculator and his ticket stubs and worked out exactly how much he's spent. But Gary knows this for sure: if it wasn't for Leeds United, he'd be a rich man.

Since the beginning of 1968, he hasn't missed a single game. Whether it was down the road, or on the other side of the world; he was there. Always. Well, except once, in 1981, when a strike by Spanish air traffic control thwarted his meticulously-timed plan to follow Leeds from a pre-season tour in Spain to a friendly in Toronto. But Gary's not bitter. He's no completist, he just follows Leeds. With the zest of a stalker. "I've been everywhere in Europe," he says. "Greece. Malaysia. The Philippines. Australia. China. America. South Africa. Scandinavia…"

The flipside of Gary's devotion is a pathological hatred of Manchester United. He hasn't uttered their name in 30 years, he reckons. And if the love of Leeds has cost the decorator dear, then ill-will hasn't been cheap either.

"If you've got a red wall, I'll paint it white, free of charge," he says. "That's my offer. I've had loads of people take me up on it. But I'm not totally stupid though," he adds. "I'll only do one coat for nothing."

TWO PINTS OF LAGER AND BAGGIES OF CRISPS

The Albion is pretty much everything a West Brom fan could want from a match-day boozer. It's the Hawthorns in pub form; an inn crammed with memorabilia, with a giant club crest over the door and toilets marked Baggie Boys and Baggie Babes.

It's the perfect place to sink a pint or two before a home game. Or at least it would be if it wasn't slap bang in the East End of London, a full 130 miles away from West Bromwich.

When landlord Dave arrived it was the plain old Duke of Sussex. "I wanted to do something off-the-wall with it," he says, "and you can't get more off-the-wall than a West Brom pub in London. Loads of the locals are Arsenal fans so I used old programmes to create a Highbury corner by the dartboard to placate them. That helped."

Word has spread about Dave's displaced temple to West Brom. Now it's filling up with all kinds of keepsakes. "Lorry drivers will stop by and say "ere, put this up" and hand over a Scunthorpe pennant or something," he says. They're all welcome, whoever they support. But there's one lot that steadfastly stay away. "I think we've only had one Wolves fan in here," chuckles Dave. "He still comes. He's a regular from the Duke of Sussex days. The day we first opened he arrived as usual and stopped dead outside. He looked at the sign for about four minutes. His face was a picture."

"AT FIRST THE LOCALS THOUGHT I WAS STARK RAVING MAD."

ETERNALLY 3PM

"I'VE BEEN TO AT LEAST THREE GAMES WHERE I WAS THE ONLY ONE WATCHING."

There's something that David wants to get straight, right from the off. He may be the FA librarian, he may average 200 matches a season, his life may be almost entirely consumed by the game, but he's not an anorak. Absolutely. Not at all. "I do wear one though," he concedes. "It's just the thing if you're out in the cold and rain all the time."

On the day we speak, David had seen a total 4,731 games. It'll be more by now. That might be a record, no-one really knows. But if there's anyone else who crams in football every single day of every single week, except those tumbleweed Thursdays when there's not a ball to be seen kicked, well, David doesn't know about him. Surely the thrill must have gone? "No, it's exactly the same for me now as when I started going in 1960," he says. "Most of the games I go to, I'm the first person in the ground. It's ridiculous really, after all these years."

Champions League, Premier League, women's league, Sunday league: he's seen them all. Sometimes all alone in the stands.

Let's forget that best-match worst-match guff. What was the oddest? "Oh there've been plenty. Only the other day I was at one where the linesman was on crutches. But Wandsworth Police Station versus Uruguay in 1990, that takes some beating. It was 3-1 to Uruguay. A good result for those police lads."

SHIRT SHRIFT

Mick is the Imelda Marcos of football shirts. She hoarded shoes; he loads up his wardrobe with replica tops. The hanger rail at home groans under the weight of them all: Birmingham City or England; home, away or third strip; vintage or modern, classic-design or hideous fashion error; he's got the lot. And he wears the lot too, night after night, down at the pub. "This guy turned to me the other day and said 'Blimey, how many have you got?'."

Enough to make Liberace look like a man struggling for a change of clothes, that's the answer. Mick could turn up at the pub 85 times on the trot and still not have to wear the same shirt twice.

This tiny private museum to football fashion boasts 53 Birmingham tops alone. His favourite is a plain royal blue one from the early 1970s. And the worst? "That's easy: the one splattered with white from the early 1990s when we were sponsored by Triton. It looks like it's been worn in a paintball game. Do I wear it? Absolutely, though I save it for special occasions, like fancy dress parties."

He doesn't just stockpile shirts though. He also has a range of mugs from all the clubs that Birmingham have played. And at the bottom of the wardrobe, Mick keeps his collection of programmes and t-shirts bearing earthily-worded sentiments about Aston Villa. There's also stash of leaflets from the club announcing new kits. "I used to frame them," he says. "I don't do that anymore. That was a bit sad."

"I WEAR A DIFFERENT ONE EVERY NIGHT OF THE WEEK DOWN AT THE PUB."

HERR, THERE AND EVERYWHERE

"I JUST FELL IN LOVE THERE AND THEN."

Somewhere in the workmanlike German city of Duisburg, there's a woman whose hatred of Nottingham must surely rival anything conjured up in Leicester or Derby.

She's the ex-wife of long-distance Forest fan Eberhard, and the East Midlands club wrecked her marriage. "One day she said to me 'you love Forest more than me'," says the man universally known at the City Ground as Ebby, "and I said 'yes, it's true'. We split up and I've never seen her again. And I don't care." He really doesn't: Ebby's got other matters on his mind. Forest, chiefly.

His weekly pilgrimage to Britain begins with a twenty minute drive from his home in Duisburg to the airport at Düsseldorf. It's a journey Ebby knows well, he's made it more than 700 times since he first saw Forest in 1978. "I'd read about Forest in a German football paper," he explains. "I decided to book a flight to see them play Liverpool. I heard it had sold out, but I bought a ticket off a tout for £120."

The pleasure is still with him, more than 1,000 games later. "On the flight home, I'm already looking forward to the next game," he says. "I'd never give it up. I've flown over for Forest matches when I have had a fever. I'd rather finish my life than miss a game."

SEATS YOU SIR

In his defence, he thought it was a wind up. And who could blame him? After all, it's not every day a bloke from Bury gets a call from someone claiming to be the president of UEFA.

So Gordon slammed down the phone in a pithy peal of profanities. It was only a fortnight later that he discovered it really had been Lennart Johansson on the line, and he really had been crowned UEFA's Best Supporter. Still. Despite that tirade.

The award was recognition for a dogged pursuit of cash for troubled Bury, a club that found itself almost poor enough for the proverbial church mouse to take pity upon. Someone came up with the idea of selling space for names on the Gigg Lane seats. Gordon set about whipping up interest on the web and in the press with a near-evangelical zeal. Soon they'd flogged name tags on 16,000 seats. Not bad, seeing as Bury have only got 12,000. And so Gordon found himself at a glitzy gala dinner in Monaco among the gathered great and the good of the game: a Shaker among movers, you might say.

"I picked up the trophy, sat down and got a pat on my back," he says. "This voice said 'well done, mon ami," he says. "I looked round and it was Zinedine Zidane. But to be honest I was more interested in the Bury result. We'd been playing Boston and it was the first game I'd missed in five years."

"I GOT THE PILOT TO FIND OUT THE SCORE DURING THE FLIGHT BACK HOME."

THE HORNIEST MAN IN ENGLAND

"I JUST FILLED UP."

On the day his life changed forever, John drove to Liverpool, shoved a bugle up his jumper and strode into Goodison Park. Eighty minutes into the match, with his beloved Sheffield Wednesday 2-0 up, he risked the wrath of the stewards by pulling out the instrument he'd learned as a cub scout, and blasting a foghorn fanfare of the Owls' anthem Aida. Cue uproar in the away end.

John was back home in the bath when manager Trevor Francis rang, and told him the club could afford to buy a drum or two, if he was interested. And so the Wednesday band was born.

Three years later, with Hillsborough the undisputed home of the horn, John was on the M62 when he took another entirely unexpected call. It was the FA, asking him if he could play for England. He was overwhelmed. "Being a fan and getting the call-up must be equally as good as being a player."

It was Rome that sealed the reputation of the England band. England played Italy; the band played the Great Escape; 14,000 travelling England fans joined in, and didn't stop all night.

The repertoire numbers 137 tunes now, though they never rehearse. "The guy on the terrace isn't Pavarotti," says John, "and nor are we the Hallé Orchestra."

STRINGER THE WINGER

He's tried and he's tried, but Jim can't remember much about the first time he saw Rochdale play. It was sunny, he recalls. And he sat on the grass with his dad. That's about it. But whatever happened, whenever it was, it was enough: his life has been entwined with his humble hometown rugby league team ever since.

A littler Jim was a ball boy for the reserves. Then he helped out the kitman. He edited the programme and ran the fanzine and was the tannoy announcer for a while too. He runs the club website now, and the supporters' association. And he's on the marketing committee.

But in his Hornets-infested CV, there's one job that eclipses all the others. "At 16, I had a trial for the club," he says. "I was a winger, a very slow winger, but a winger all the same and I got into the under 17s. The day you pull on the shirt for the first time is unbelievable when you're a fan too. I had to go and look at myself in the mirror, I couldn't believe it was me."

It was, it really was. But not for long. At the age of 19, a career-ending injury stretchered him off the pitch and dumped him back in the stands. No matter: He's happy there too. Whatever the job. Well almost. He's not bothered about being Chairman, "I'm not interested in meeting and greeting." So that leaves just one last position: Boss. "Well, I do have a coaching certificate," he says, after a wistful pause, "but I'm afraid putting on the manager's tracksuit is beyond me."

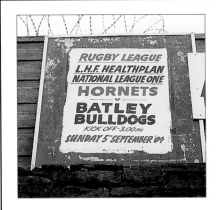

RUGBY LEAGUE
L.H.F. HEALTHPLAN
NATIONAL LEAGUE ONE
HORNETS
v
BATLEY
BULLDOGS
KICK OFF - 3.00 PM
SUNDAY 5 SEPTEMBER '04

"I GET RIBBED ALL THE TIME ABOUT WHETHER I'LL END UP AS CHAIRMAN."

ALL HANDS TO THE PUMPS

"I DON'T GET TO WATCH ANY MORE."

Three o'clock on a Saturday afternoon, and die-hard Wimbledon fan Ronan is where he always is at the defining hour of his week: Down at the football. He's an ever-present at home games, a fixture at every fixture, even though he never sees a single kick of the ball.

Ronan, a season ticket holder in the old days of Wimbledon, is now a barman at the club's new home at the Kingsmeadow Stadium. It's all hands to the pumps with the reborn Dons these days. Ronan's ended up on the ones that draw beer.

From behind the bar he doesn't get to see much of the action. "We've gone 75 matches unbeaten and I think I've seen about six or seven of them. I can't see the pitch from the bar but when you hear 3,000 people cheer you can tell that something's happened."

A lot's happened at AFC Wimbledon, of course. "We're a strange capitalist-communist-democratic organisation these days," says Ronan. "We own and run the club. I said I'd do any shifts in the bar as long as it wasn't during the game. My first shift? During the game."

Bar duties at the Kingsmeadow mean Ronan hardly ever gets to go to away matches anymore. "But I did go to one last year," he says. "We all went for a drink before kick-off, but there were far too many of us so I jumped over the bar and helped out." What, during the game too? "God no, at ten to three I said 'forget this, I'm off'."

VILLA ARE THE KINGS

Mountfield and
Daley sink Albion

F.C. - 1985/86

WEMBLEY WONDERS
MATCH OF THE DECADE
This was a tie-break
final: a dead heat in
the

MARK'S HOLIDAY VILLA

The way Mark sees it, it's just like Mass. "Some people go to church," he reasons. "I go down to the Villa." And like any true believer, Mark is devoted. Not obsessed, mind you: devoted. No, actually: scrub that. He is obsessed too.

Mark's version of morning worship has taken him to every domestic Villa fixture since September 1980. Breaking his leg in 1986 couldn't keep him away, so the unfortunate matter of a pre-booked family holiday in 2000 wasn't going to come between him and the chance to see Villa in Europe. Well, Villa in the Intertoto Cup.

"We were all going away to Weymouth," says the Birmingham draughtsman. "We left on the Friday. I came back on the Saturday for the Marila Príbram match. We got through. I went back on holiday and by the Wednesday I was flying out to Spain to see Villa against Celta Vigo." Still, Weymouth's lovely at that time of year. And Mark's wife was understanding. "She did have a few words, though" he says.

His unbroken run of Villa matches now stretches to 1,151. And win, lose or draw, it's the same routine after each one. Come Monday, Mark draws the Villa curtains in his Villa-wallpapered home, cuts out the match report from The Sun or the Daily Star and sticks it carefully into a scrapbook. He's got 26 now. Every religion needs a ritual.

"IT'S A KIND OF RELIGION FOR ME."

49

ONE WEDDING AND A FUNERAL

"HE'D HAVE BEEN CHUFFED TO BITS."

They'd go to the game together, Mick and his father. It was a dad and son thing, a ritual which had survived the passing of the years and the generational force that steadily pulls the child from the parent. Mick (centre stage in the picture) may have left home, grown up and had kids of his own, but when Saturday came it was the same as it ever was. George would stay over the night before, then they'd drive up to watch Charlton.

They split up as usual outside The Valley, that day in March 2000; father to his seat and son to his, with his own lads Gavin and Neil in tow. It was a dismal match in an otherwise intoxicating season. But half-an-hour before the final whistle Mick's attention was caught by a flurry of activity in the opposite stand.

George had died of a heart attack. "That's the way he'd have chosen to have gone," says Mick. "Down at The Valley. If I could see him now, he'd say 'how did we get on?'." How did they get on? "We lost. It was a bloody awful game."

Charlton kept George's seat vacant for the rest of the season. Mick was touched by that. "On the last game, I went and sat in it," he says. Four years later, Mick got married in the ground where his father had died. The bride and groom had their photo taken down on the pitch. "I looked over to that seat of his," says Mick, "and imagined him sitting there watching. He'd have been chuffed to bits."

RHYME OF PASSION

He's played Glastonbury. He's taken to the stage at the Royal Festival Hall. And he's appeared at the Cheltenham Festival of Literature. Crispin has done the lot, apart from the big one: Stamford Bridge. That's the gig the performance poet craves the most.

"It would be daunting," he says. "But I'm hoping to do it one day. Reading out poetry right in the centre circle before kick off or at half time, with 40,000 people there. I like the idea of it spilling out of a crackly tannoy. Or I'd take a megaphone. I like megaphones."

The qwertysomething Chelsea fan is part of the Stroud's stanza squad, the United Rhymers who – last time anyone checked - form the only known collection of football poets in the world. "They are funny words to put together, football and poetry," concedes Crispin, "but I'd always written poetry and I'd always loved football, so it seemed natural.

"We just want to make people smile and make people think. It's football, culture. We remind people that football fans are not a bunch of racist yobbos. We're all kinds of people.

"There is poetry in everything, and what we do is not that different from the way fans make up chants on the spot. Football is a fantastic outlet, it's a release. And writing about it is a release too."

"WE'RE SWAPPING SHIRTS WITH SHAKESPEARE, THAT'S HOW WE SEE IT.

IT TAKES ONE TO TANGO

"IT WAS -7C OR SOMETHING AND I TOOK MY SHIRT OFF"

The future might be bright, but it's not orange. Not anymore, not for Paul, Sheffield Wednesday's celebrated Tango Man. He's had enough of painting himself the colour of carrots, even if it did turn him into a terrace icon and bring him fan mail from as far away as Zimbabwe. It's too much of a pain to put on and get off afterwards, you see.

But more than 10 years since he first shivered shirtlessly through a match, he's still whipping his top off in sub-zero temperatures.

Why, for pity's sake? "It's a big buzz," he says, simply. And, orange or not, he's still standing up to drink in the chant that's followed him for a decade: "Tango, Tango, Tango."

It all started in 1991. Wednesday were playing Derby. On a freezing cold afternoon Paul took his shirt off and fame came calling. "The ITV cameras picked up on it." It was Crystal Palace fans who christened him. It was something to do with a big orange hand he had on. "It just went on from there," he says.

No, he doesn't feel the chill. "People say I must be freezing, but it doesn't bother me. When you're in the middle of a lot of people, you get a bit of warmth off them. And I like the winter, it's the heat I don't like. When everyone else takes off their shirts at the end of the season, I wear a coat."

THE BULL THAT GREW UP A TIGER

You can swap political parties, walk out on your wife and capriciously change your tune on the burning issues of the day. But in the opposing camps of rugby, swapping sides is roughly on a par with telling the Taliban you enjoy a drink, a dance and a spot of mixed beardless Twister of an evening.

So Nick is a rugby rarity: a fan who switched codes, ditching his childhood love of union for a born-again passion for league. You can count the number of supporters who've made the same journey on the fingers on Captain Hook's most magnetic hand.

Nick followed Leicester Tigers until he met the woman who became his wife. "Most people when they get married gain a mother-in-law," says Bradford Bulls' most vociferous convert. "I gained my wife's passion for rugby league."

The Bulls got trounced the first game he saw. "But the intensity, the speed, it was so different to rugby union. I think it's a fantastic game."

Having belatedly seen the light, Nick made sure his son knows which side of rugby's Berlin Wall he belongs on. "One of my proudest moments was taking my son to his first Bulls game," he says. "He was 10 days old."

"THE FIRST MATCH I SAW, THE BULLS GOT TROUNCED."

BETTER RED THAN DEAD

"I'D NEVER LET UNITED DOWN BY GOING TO WATCH ANYONE ELSE, LIKE MAN CITY."

There's not a great deal that Norman wants from life any more, but at 82, he's got one last all-consuming ambition. Like a test batsman on the brink of his maiden century, he's hellbent on hitting 100. It's not the anticipation of a telegram from the Queen that keeps him going; he just can't bear the thought of dying, and missing a match at Old Trafford.

That's quite understandable: he hasn't skipped one for the last 78 years. "It's true," he says. "I first went when I was four in 1926. And I haven't missed one since. My dad took me every week. We'd watch the first team one Saturday, then the reserves the next."

Things were different in those days. Manchester City were top dogs in town, and today's Theatre of Dreams™ was just a dream. "Only one stand at Old Trafford had a roof back then," says Norman. "If it had been raining, my mum would do her fruit when we got back soaking. 'You two, you're mad,' she'd say, 'I don't know what you're doing standing there for an hour and a half in the rain.'"

It's comfier these days of course and Old Trafford is now like a home from home for Norman. "Inside me, I feel like part of the family," he says. "God willing I'll live until I'm 100. I don't want to miss anything. And if I fall ill, they'll have to take me down there on a stretcher."

THE MAN THAT KILLED DAVE BEESTON

Dave Beeston died the kind of death we'd all wish for ourselves: quick, clean and painless, and reassuringly free of screaming. He went willingly, in the offices of a solicitor, in a deed poll demise that saw him instantly reborn as Dave Burnley.

That was the easy part; it was the next task that was hard. "I went home and said "Dad, I've changed my name"," he says. "I can still see him there cooking, the pans rattling away, staring back at me. He'd had little respect for me at the time. But I think at that point he realised supporting Burnley wasn't just a hobby, it was my life."

It was a life almost wrecked by the Clarets. Dave twice caught pneumonia while sleeping rough after missing the last train home from away games. And at 16, he got expelled from school for skipping his mock O levels to catch Burnley at Chelsea.

Six years later, as Burnley were relegated, an emotionally-bruised Dave strode decisively into that firm of lawyers. "It's just like women changing their name when they get married," he insists. "It's a statement of love and loyalty."

Dave's a dad himself now. He named his daughter Clarette. "I wanted to call her Clarette Anne Bilou Burnley, but her mum said she wasn't having her daughter named after a Jungle Book character."

"MY PARENTS WEREN'T VERY HAPPY, TO BE HONEST."

61

HAPPY BIRTHDAY DEAR, I'M OFF OUT

"I'D RATHER STICK PINS IN MY EYES THAN WATCH RUGBY UNION."

It wasn't meant to turn out this way, it just kind of happened. One game turned into another game; one season blended into another season. And all of a sudden the man they call Spelly on the terraces at Swinton had seen every game the club has played for the last quarter of a century. "I didn't set out to," he says. "I didn't say 'I'm not going to miss a match for 25 years. But every now and again I'd think: 'well, that's another season,' and another season, and another season."

Now here he is, on his silver anniversary of unstinting devotion to a team that frankly haven't always deserved it. "It's never boring being a Swinton fan," says John. "It might be frustrating, it might be joyous, but it's never dull." Even if it was, Spelly's devotion to Swinton probably wouldn't wane. He lives for rugby, Spelly does.

Maybe he loves it just a bit too much. "I've missed my girfriend's last three birthdays," he announces, without a hint of sheepishness. "She says to me "what are we doing on my birthday?" and I say "it all depends on the fixtures".

The fixtures have wedged England A games between him and her for the last two years. And this year? "Great Britain v Australia," he says. "The big one. I can't miss that".

GET WITH THE PROGRAMMES

It was an inheritance, of sorts. When Steve was a kid, he found a stack of his dad's old Spurs programmes stashed in a wardrobe like pornography. Leafing through them was a time-tunnel peek into the seasons he'd never see; Steve was transfixed, and the collection was soon his.

"It kind of went from there," he says, downplaying the long labour of love that turned that bundle of booklets into an irreplaceable archive of Tottenham keepsakes. He's got several thousand programmes now, all bound up, and neatly filed away in his study. The oldest ones date from before the First World War. "But it's relatively complete back to the late 1950s," he says. Relatively complete? "Yeah, there's a handful missing. The quest is to complete the set.

"It doesn't take over my life. I'm a fan primarily, not a collector. Some collectors don't even go to games", says Steve with a dismissive snort. "A few years ago I met this guy buying a programme. He told me he always bought three copies of the programme – one to read, one to keep, and one in case the others get damaged." It's a cautionary tale, he grins.

So why does he do it? "It's like your record of that day," he says. "Beyond that, well I don't want to open that dark, dank box of why men collect things. I've read articles about that and it doesn't make for easy reading."

"BUT I'M A RELATIVELY BALANCED INDIVIDUAL."

ONE FOR THE LADIES

"OBVIOUSLY THERE'S A VAST DIFFERENCE IN THE FOOTBALL."

If Coventry City were a narcotic, Kev would be loaded from dawn to dusk. He's hooked, addicted, habituated, and all kinds of other stoned synonyms from the thesaurus: his life, simply put, is consumed by Cov.

Kev doesn't just follow the first team home and away. He also follows Coventry reserves. Home and away. And Coventry City Ladies. Home and away. It's not unusual for him to rack up 800 miles or more a week in hot pursuit of anything involving a ball and several Sky Blue shirts.

"I quite enjoy travelling," he says. He needs to: One afternoon he'll be among thousands watching Coventry's first XI lock horns with one of the grand old names of English football; the next he'll be cheering on the CCFC women in a park. Two days later he'll have followed the second string to a rickety ground in a town they forgot to knock down. "It's a Jekyll and Hyde life," he admits. "But I celebrate all the goals."

"On the night Spain played England in Madrid, I saw Coventry reserves play West Ham at Dagenham. I could have gone to Spain, in fact, but y'know. We scored first and I went mental. There were only 60 people in the stand but it upset them all. They spent the rest of the game staring at me."

LANCASHIRE, LA, LA, LA

Like a sudden, rib-shuddering belch, inspiration can strike at any time, and often comes in the unlikeliest places. Paul Simon composed Homeward Bound on Widnes station, while waiting for the milk train back to London. Lennon and McCartney bashed out From Me To You on a coach to Shrewsbury. And Ian was in a pub in Southport when he dreamed up The Scarf My Father Wore, the song that became the Stockport County rabble-rouser.

"I can play it for you if you like," offers the man they call The Godfather Of The Cheadle End. *"He wants to hear the anthem,"* whispers Ian to his wife, as he clatters around on the other end of the line, looking for the CD.

And here it is: a portentous stab of Jaws-style strings which segues into a soaring crowd chant that bears the lines: "It's forever being beautiful, and the colour's white and blue. I wore it proud around my neck, at Chesterfield and Crewe. My father was a County fan, like my grandfather before. And at Edgeley Park, I love to wear the scarf my father wore."

Ian's muse stuck around after he'd penned The Scarf My Father Wore. Over the last four decades, he's written around 30 Stockport songs. But only this one wound up the tune the team run out to at home games. So how did he feel, hearing it for the first time over the tannoy? "Woooof," he exhales, making a noise like an especially hungry man spotting a Sunday roast.

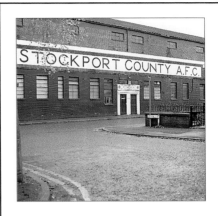

"IT'S OUR ANTHEM."

THE STICKER BOOK THAT STUCK

EDDIE GRAY | TERRY HIBBITT | NORMAN HUNTER
PETER LORIMER | PAUL MADELEY | PAUL REANEY

"I WAS SIX AND THAT STICKER ALBUM WAS MY WHOLE WORLD."

It was quite a year, 1970. The Beatles broke up. Jimi Hendrix and Joni Mitchell died. And little Bob got a sticker book. The Wonderful World of Soccer Stars, it was called, and it had an immediate, mesmeric effect.

At first, he was content to collect the stickers. Then he started updating the player biographies, and never quite got round to stopping.

Maybe the story would have ended there, with a solitary man in his forties merrily charting the steady journey into obscurity of the crowd-pleasers and cloggers of yesteryear. But then the internet age arrived.

Bob is now the webmaster of an entire site devoted to the 1970/71 season. It's a sprawling love letter to a lost age of football, crammed with minute detail and pictures of men with ill-advised facial hair.

"It's become my life, soul and purpose," says Bob, with a bashful laugh. "There's no adequate answer why. It's probably diagnosable." Perhaps it is: Bob didn't see a single game in 1970/71. "Not one," he smiles. "I'm so envious when people tell me they saw Ken Wagstaff or someone else from that era play."

ALL YOU NEED IS LOVE (AND A TICKET)

The March winds howled, the icy rain lashed down. Maybe there was fog and lightning too. You get the picture: it was an evening to stay indoors. Yet in the streetlight glow of small-hours Newcastle, Swindon fan Rob sank back in the patio chair he'd placed outside St James' Park and settled down for his one wretched night in town.

As city breaks go, it left something to be desired. But Rob gave neither a hoot nor a monkey's about the weather: he was simply content to be at the head of an as-yet unformed queue for the last 200 tickets for United's match with Swindon. "It was one of those bizarre things you do," says Rob, with the tone of a man who actually doesn't find his behaviour in the slightest bit bizarre. "That possibility of a ticket was all the incentive I needed."

A few days later, Rob was back in the north east, only to see Swindon mauled 7-1. It's enough to make a man question why he bothers. But it's all for the love of the game.

And Rob does love it: there's no suppose about it. Of the last 1,009 games Swindon have played, he's seen all 1,009. Even the ones he feared he'd miss. Like Shrewsbury in 1987, when he caught a taxi from Gloucester after his train broke down. "I had no choice," he says. He also had no cash. "I told the cabbie he'd double his money if he waited outside the ground. He got £80. It must have made his night."

"YOU DO IT BECAUSE YOU LOVE IT, I SUPPOSE."

DIAMONDS ARE A BLOKE'S BEST FRIEND

"THEY'RE A MAJOR CONTRIBUTION TO ROAD SAFETY."

In a tribe, identity is everything. In New Zealand, the Maori tattoo their faces. In Ethiopia, Karo men scar their chests. In Burma, Padaung women stretch their necks with brass rings. And in west London, a bunch of Harlequins fans wear multi-coloured chefs' trousers.

The Diamond Geezers were born two or three years ago, when someone spotted a shop-window displaying a pair of slacks that could induce a migraine with a single glance. Harlequin trousers, said the label. It was enough to clinch a sale, and spark a craze.

Pretty soon you could barely move for them down at The Stoop.

"The club always had a reputation of being posh and stuffy," says Diamond Geezer Duncan. "We wanted to get away from all that, and the Barbour jacket and club tie business." He felt stupid the first time, catching the train to Twickenham in a pair of strides that would make a clown scoff.

But he got over it. And daft as they may be, these Cor-Blimiest of all trousers have their uses. "We go abroad and drink a huge amount and people fall over in the road," says Duncan. "But nobody's been run over while wearing them."

THE OTHER TOON ARMY

The heat, that's the worst bit; the stifling heat of the all-day sun in the Test match towns of Australia, South Africa and the Caribbean. It's bad enough for the rest of England's Barmy Army, their exposed guts burning an angry shade of crimson in the scorching stands. But for the two men sweltering beside them in furry Sylvester the Cat and Pink Panther outfits, a day at the cricket can be almost unbearable.

There are times when Jim and Kev don't think they can take it. But no matter how high the Mercury creeps up the thermometer, the fancy dress costumes stay on.

"That's the rule," says Jim, the Sheffield copper in the Sylvester suit. "Even the heads can't come off until we get back to the hotel. In Melbourne in 2002 it was 37°C. We were looking at each other and thinking 'how are we going to last?' But we did.

"My suit is worse than Kev's though," he adds. "It's half-black, his is pink. Mine's even hotter inside."

It's a moot point: both wind-up sweatier than the jockstrap of a feverish sumo wrestler. Maybe that's why Jim and Kev so quickly mastered the art of drinking in costume. "You can get a bottle in through the eyehole," says Jim. Perfect.

"IT LOOKS LUDICROUS ON TV, BUT IT DOES THE TRICK."

JEREMY'S DREAM JOB

"IT'S AN EMOTIONAL ATTACHMENT, NOT A FINANCIAL ONE."

Like Martin Luther King, Jeremy had a dream. Unlike Martin Luther King, it was about the World Cup.

It was the summer of 1998; West Ham had just invited him to be their tannoy man for the coming season. "I'd said 'no thanks' at first," says the BBC sports journalist. "But then I had this recurring dream that England won the World Cup in France and Rio Ferdinand scored the winning goal, and the new season would start with me on the Upton Park pitch saying 'please welcome the player who scored goal that won us the cup'."

So he changed his mind. But unlike Martin Luther King, Jeremy's dream didn't come true. "Rio didn't even get a kick in France '98. The first home game was Manchester United and I found myself announcing David Beckham, the man who you could say had just lost us the World Cup. And his name unleashed this incredible sea of hatred."

Jeremy's been at West Ham for seven seasons now. He doesn't need the work, he says, he's there because he loves the club. "It's not really a bright career move to be a sports presenter who is unavailable every other weekend."

A NUNN'S HABIT

Like all the best stories, it started with a boy and a girl. Two boys and a girl, to be exact, and a cat and a dog, plus a firm of builders. And all of them named after Crystal Palace in one way or another.

Paul was already the proud owner of a moggy called Crystal, a mutt called Palace and a firm known as Eagle Builders when his daughter was born. You may be able to take an educated guess at what followed. Paula Barbara Crystal Palace Nunn was christened to a chorus of chuckles in church. "Even the vicar couldn't stop laughing," says Paul. "But you hear a lot of people naming their girls Chelsea."

When her brother PJ came along, Paul couldn't resist a replay. "I leaned in as the registrar was noting his name and quietly made an addition." His girlfriend hadn't heard. Then she was handed a birth certificate that read Paul Junior Edward Palace Nunn.

"She rolled her eyes but the registrar smiled and said 'it's done now'." By now Paul was on a roll. Enter Edward Michael Simon Jordan Nunn, named – curiously – after the Selhurst Park chairman.

Paul insists he won't mind if his kids' ardour for the club proves no match for his own. And if they wind up supporting Brighton? "Well," he says, after a moment's consideration, "then they'll have to move home."

"I THOUGHT I'D BE ORIGINAL."

WHAT DO YOU THINK OF IT SO FAR?

"WE DID THAT EVERY WEEK FOR AN ENTIRE SEASON."

Glen is getting ready to go to the match. He puts on his scarf, his dirty old mac and flat cap, pins on his rosette, pops on his Eric Morecambe glasses, sticks a pipe in mouth and he's out the door. There's a similar ritual happening at homes all over Morecambe. The Erics will be out in force at Christie Park today.

It's been like this, on and off, since Glen's stag do. He could have gone to Amsterdam, Dublin or Prague; he chose Barnet. Glen and his mates drove down dressed up as cartoon northerners. It kind of went from there, with the ekky-thump get-up refined into charity shop tributes to England's greatest comedian.

They save the dressing up for the big occasions. In between, there are other things to be getting on with. Like drawing spoof announcements from tannoy announcers at away games. "It was always for our friend Steve Downs. He was congratulated on his golden wedding, his BAFTA award for a short animated film, a successful Arctic expedition, completing the Inca trail and becoming the first male referee in the North West ladies' netball league. Plus loads more. None of it was true," says Glen.

ALL THINGS BRIGHTON BEAUTIFUL

Love. Sex. Emotional turbulence. These are the time-honoured themes of the tunes that clutter up the charts from week to week. So Attila the Stockbroker's plan to gatecrash the Top 20 with a song about a thwarted planning application seemed the musical equivalent of a hopeful punt at goal from the halfway line. By a blind pensioner. With a gammy leg. In adverse weather.

Brighton's poet-in-residence was in the PA box of Albion's ridiculously ill-appointed temporary home at Withdean when he was struck by the idea of updating The Piranhas' ska floor-filler Tom Hark. "The Piranhas were Brighton through-and-through," he says. "It always seems ironic when other teams play Tom Hark to celebrate scoring against us."

An irritated Attila reclaimed it for Albion, modifying the words into a rabble-rousing call for a new ground at nearby Falmer:
For years the planning process has dragged on and on. A paralytic snail wouldn't take that long. We're stuck in an athletics track we really hate. Like playing in Albania Division Eight.

Attila was in his bedroom when he turned on the Radio One Chart Show for the first time in almost 30 years to find his hastily-assembled band Seagulls Ska had reached number 17 with their literal take on stadium rock. He was, naturally, delighted.

"APPARENTLY WE OUTSOLD ELVIS ON AMAZON THAT WEEK."

THE GROUNDS MAN

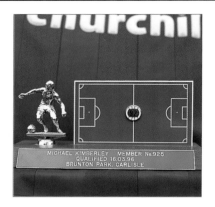

"I LIKE THE STADIUMS AND THE BANTER."

It was just a fling. A one-off. It meant nothing to him really. Mike was away from home, and he needed a bit of action. So he headed for the back streets of Barrow, and found himself handing over his hard-earned cash.

Until then, Crystal Palace's Mr Reliable had been completely faithful. But that moment of betrayal at the turnstiles of the Holker Street Stadium turned him into one of the swingers of the sports world: the ground-hoppers. Soon he'd clocked up more footballing infidelities: A match at Walsall; another at Peterborough; and away days in Wigan and Rochdale to add to all the stadiums he'd been to with Palace.

By now he was insatiable, and in March 1996, Mike walked into his 92nd league ground: Carlisle's Brunton Park. United drew 1-1 with Shrewsbury, but Mike wasn't especially interested in the scoreline. He was just happy to have finished the 92 Club set. "The results are of no consequence," he says.

He's let it slip a little of late. Relegations and promotions mean he needs more grounds to complete the current 92. "But the family don't mind, if I take them with me," he says. "I used to say 'why don't we go to the Lake District for the weekend. And maybe we can stop off at Preston on the way'."

THE FAX OF LIFE

Theropod dinosaurs. Post-Socratic Philosophy. The Art and Architecture of Constantinople, AD 330-1453. None of these were Duncan's specialised subject on Mastermind. No, when the lights dimmed and he settled into the most famous black chair in TV history, he fielded questions on The History of Halifax Rugby League Football Club.

It was a canny move, getting quizzed on your lifelong love; Duncan scored 17, with no passes. "I got them all right," he admits, with a blush you can almost hear. "They were slightly easier than I thought they would be."

That's quite possible: Duncan brushed up on Fax facts for two hours a night for three months. "My wife got a bit fed up of sitting in bed asking me questions at the end of the evening," he says. "But it was worth it. Once I got on, in a strange masochistic way, I found it quite enjoyable."

It was even more enjoyable when he realised he'd won his heat. But Duncan didn't get too carried away; he's a down-to-earth sort of chap. He didn't even watch his Mastermind debut.

"I don't suppose many did," he says. "England were playing Portugal in Euro 2004. I switched over every now and again though, when the game got dull. Just to see how I was getting on."

I THINK I'D REVISED TO A DEEPER LEVEL."

DING, WHEN YOU'RE WINNING

"THE CUP GAME IS OVER BUT THE EXCITEMENT'S NOT."

Take it easy, the doctor said. Relax, unwind, slow down. After years of rushing around, a fatigued Brian had just suffered the grim wake-up call of a heart attack.

Get yourself a new interest, his GP advised. So Brian decided to take a trip down to his local non-league club. "Nothing exciting ever happens down there," friends had joked, as Brian joined the small knot of regulars at the home ground of lowly Yeading.

At first it all went to plan. Nothing much exciting happened. Then the Londoners got promoted. Soon afterwards they'd stormed into a huge lead in the Ryman League. And then they went on a FA Cup run that brought the part-timers face to face with the multi-millionaires of Newcastle United.

"The thing was not to get too excited," laughs Brian, "and then we went and got Newcastle. It was unbelievable. We were all over the TV and in every paper going." The match itself was tremendous, he says, even though the gallant gaggle of electricians and plasterers were knocked out.

Life's settled down again now. A little. "We've still got to win the league," says Brian down the phone, as the Ding take on Chelmsford. And to the muffled sound of cheering, Yeading score. "Wha-hey," he yells.

YORK THIS WAY

Time, according to that trite old saying, is the great healer. York City are something of a pick-me-up too, or at least they were for Keith. When his wife Gloria died four years ago, Keith found comfort and solace in the team he'd supported since he was a lad. "I think I used it as something to get me going again and get my mind off things," he says.

'Get yourself to Bootham Crescent' might not be a tip plucked from the Big Book Of Dealing With Grief, but it seemed to work for Keith. The trouble is, he lives in Portsmouth, a full 278 miles away from York. Still, that hasn't stopped him. If the traffic's good, he can drive there and back in eight hours, and still make last orders at his local. "I've managed to get a couple of the regulars to come up with me."

Keith quit Yorkshire in the sixties to join the navy. But no matter where he was in the world, he'd find time to continue his homemade history of York City. He'd been diligently compiling it since 1965. It was a real labour of love, which now lies on the seabed in the south Atlantic. Keith served in the Falklands War; his ship was HMS Sheffield. "The Exocet hit completely without warning," he remembers. "I was sitting in my working area when there was an almighty bang and debris all around us. There were three of us were in that room, only two of us got out. Everything I had was lost. I've been trying to put that diary together again. But it's hard, there are lots of bits missing."

"THEY'RE ALL QUITE INTRIGUED BY IT DOWN AT THE PUB."

ACKNOWLEDGEMENTS

Thanks to the following for all their help in the research for this book, along with anyone we have forgotten to mention:

Tony Bluff; Katy Cooke (Barmy Army Travel); Dave Flett (thisisyork.co.uk); Sam Grundy (BISA); Mick Hamilton; Catherine Holmes; Clare Hubbard; Gareth Jones; Stephen O'Malley (4thegame); Andy Parsons (www.wednesdaymad.com); Chris Saunders (www.baggies.com); Ian Smith; Alan Tapp; Nick Veevers (Burnley FC); Adrian Waite; Barry Watson

A throaty Imthankingyow to Liz, Tom and Elsie Flynn.

Less guttural but equally sincere thanks to Ruth Hamilton, Gareth Jones, Rosemary Wilkinson, Alex Dawson and all the men in this book.

Hello to Pete, Sybil, Nick, Sharon, Emily and William Clay, and to Stan, wherever you are.

I'd also like to publicly acknowledge Lee Marlow's gift for thrift.

At the risk of looking like a man with few friends, I'll leave it there.

This book is dedicated to Chris and Dave Harvey, Bob and Mary Clay and to Jim Flynn

First published in 2005 by New Holland Publishers (UK) Ltd
London • Cape Town • Sydney • Auckland
www.newhollandpublishers.com

Garfield House
86-88 Edgware Road
London W2 2EA
United Kingdom

80 McKenzie Street
Cape Town 8001
South Africa

Level 1, Unit 4
14 Aquatic Drive
Frenchs Forest
NSW 2086
Australia

218 Lake Road
Northcote
Auckland
New Zealand

10 9 8 7 6 5 4 3 2 1

ISBN 1 84537 080 5

Editor: Ruth Hamilton
Editorial direction: Rosemary Wilkinson
Production: Hazel Kirkman
Designer: Paul Wright
Photographers: John Baxter, Laura Forrester, Gary Weekes

Reproduction by Modern Age, Hong Kong
Printed and bound by Star Standard Industries (PTE) Ltd, Singapore

Photographic Credits:
John Baxter: pp 2; 4; 6-7; 8; 13; 14; 18-19; 22-23; 24-25; 25-26; 30-
31; 38-39; 40-41; 42-43; 44-45; 48-49; 54-55; 56-57; 58-59; 60-61;
62-63; 66-67; 68-69; 70-71; 76-77; 82-83; 88-89; 92-93; cover –
bottom left; cover – top left; cover – bottom right

Laura Forrester: pp 5; 12; 20; 28-29; 32-33; 34-35; 36-37; 46-47; 50-
51; 52-53; 64-65; 72-73; 84-85; 86-87; 90-91

Gary Weekes: pp 10; 16; 74-75; 78-79; 80-81; cover – top right

By the same author:
Leicester 'Til We Die: The Final Season at Filbert Street
(The Leicester Mercury Group, 2002)